how to
REDUCE

and
CONTROL YOUR WEIGHT

through
SELF-HYPNOTISM

how to
REDUCE

and
CONTROL YOUR WEIGHT

through
SELF-HYPNOTISM

Sidney Petrie
in association with
Robert B. Stone

Englewood Cliffs, N.J.   PRENTICE-HALL, INC.

Dedication

To my wife Ruth, my daughter Jacqueline, and my son David, who have exerted their own very special hypnotic influence over me.

SIDNEY PETRIE

Acknowledgments

Sincere gratitude goes to the many people who have helped this book along the way, some without knowing it. They shall all go nameless except for Sally Russell, Jacqueline Wolcott, Catherine Rocks, and Lola Stone.

HOW THIS BOOK WILL HELP YOU LOOK BETTER, FEEL BETTER, AND LIVE LONGER THROUGH THE AMAZING POWER OF SELF-HYPNOSIS

Remember the day when people had to use will-power to stay on a diet? Now about all you do is push a button labeled self-hypnosis. Actually there are no such buttons, but there are such books and this is one.

New frontiers of the mind explored in the past decades have now yielded dividends beyond man's imagination. What was once an area bordering on witchcraft, that later rose to top vaudeville billing, is so well understood by science that it is now an accepted means by which people can regulate their lives.

There are as many uses for self-hypnosis as there are skills and habits both wanted and unwanted. This book specializes in eliminating one unwanted habit: gaining weight. It gives you the simple steps you can take to use self-hypnosis to change your eating habits *permanently* and forego fattening foods without so much as a conscience-stricken "I shouldn't" or a brave "I won't."

It teaches you how to obtain a deep state of self-hypnosis which is really only a deep state of relaxation. (Most people go through this state often, either when they are about to fall asleep or when they are transported by a movie or television show.) Then it teaches you to give yourself the suggestions that will correct your eating habits.

For instance, suppose you enjoy eating spaghetti and you find it impossible to resist it even though you know it is putting pounds on you that detract from your health and your looks. This book does not ask you to give up spaghetti. Instead it asks you to take a peek at yourself as you would be if you liked steak instead of spaghetti. You are the same person except for this one change. You dislike spaghetti intensely and love steak heartily. Of course you weigh less, look better. Want to be that person? It is just a few relaxations away.

Thousands have tried it and now look back on the days of diets and pills as a long nightmare. The techniques taught you step by step in this book have been successfully used by hundreds of persons in the author's hypnosis center. Here is just one dramatic example. A school teacher, 36, with a long history of pills, diets, even hospital stays, decided to try hypnosis and self-hypnosis as a last resort. She weighed 320 pounds. She had a 52 bust, 49 waist, 60 hips. Her upper arm measurement was 17 inches, her thigh 30 inches. She wore a 52 dress. She lost eight pounds that first week but more important she went to a party and here is how she reported what happened: "I wouldn't have believed it. I craved only those foods that were good for me and felt no desire for starchy foods. I had fun and lost weight." Two years later she weighed 160 pounds. She had a 38 bust, 29 waist, 40 hips, 11 upper arm, 21 thigh, and wore a 16 dress.

That was 1959. Did she gain it back? In 1964 she is down

to 135 pounds and has never once had to use willpower to pass up a morsel of food.

More important than this case history are the thousands of women who have found self-hypnosis a blessing in losing those unwanted 20 or 30 pounds and staying thin, and those thousands of men who have renewed their youthful vigor and energy by dropping a similar amount of life-shortening poundage.

If you like to punish yourself through deprivation and discipline, if you like to make a big thing over a diet and make everybody feel sorry for you, then this book is not for you. On the other hand, if you would like to eat well and eat right and lose weight without really trying, if you want to look and feel your best without sacrificing fun, then this is your day!

CONTENTS

13

how to
REDUCE

and
CONTROL YOUR WEIGHT

through
SELF-HYPNOTISM

1

STOP BUYING
A FAT PROFILE

You are having your morning coffee: The television newscaster is bringing you up to the minute on world developments. Next comes the weather. But first an announcement ... "Golden Cream, the richest and most delicious ice cream you can buy. It scoops smooth, spoons smooth, tastes smooth. Richest in vitamins, most delicious, thanks to pure natural dairy products. Buy the handy, economical quart size with the see-through top. Your pick of 24 tangy Golden Cream flavors." Perhaps you listen as the voice, dripping with melted vanilla, seeks your confidence. Perhaps you watch as the scoop descends into the creamy delight and then releases its ecstasy into your plate. Perhaps instead you walk away to clear some breakfast dishes. No matter. You are still "hooked." Through your subconscious, you become one more reason why it pays to advertise, why even the most irritating commercials get through to the most unwilling subjects and eventually motivate a product's use.

The daily carbohydrate bombardment can keep you chubby

Later in the day you will be bombarded by radio commercials, newspaper ads, billboards. Cake mixes will be held by beautiful models. Chocolate will be offered you by a friendly hand. And just in case beer couldn't be further from your thoughts, a bathing-suit clad boy and girl remind you that love and beer go in hand.

Not only advertising but those who respond to it provide the carbohydrate inducement to which you are subjected. You see and hear their enjoyment and enjoy with them even if it's just to be sociable. So it goes all during your waking hours. And if voices carry from the kitchen, where someone is enjoying a late coffee and doughnut, to the bedroom where you sleep, the carbohydrate barrage is still on.

The carbohydrate bombardment finds its target despite unlistening ears or disinterested eyes. The message travels along your nerves to the subconscious storage house where it waits patiently for an appropriate time to intrude into the conscious, along with all of the similar messages stored there since the beginning of time—your time, anyway. The subconscious is believed to be a limitless storehouse of such suggestions and impressions. It is also a very efficient storehouse in that it always responds at the right time with the material from the proper storage bin. Sometimes a name or place never quite made enough of an impression for the subconscious to instantly deliver it on a silver thought. Even then, it may come by special-delivery hours after we gave up ringing for it.

You can "jam" its message

Psychologists know more and more about the subconscious. They have found easy ways to reach it, communicate with it, and observe it react to this communication. They know now how you yourself can put your subconscious to work for you. Through simple procedures you can condition yourself to reject the carbohydrate barrage and possibly other aspects of your environment which might detract from your good health. In effect, you can "jam" the propaganda beamed at you and prevent it from motivating you to prefer fattening foods. You are then able to talk up your own commercials, speak to yourself about the things you would like to like and why you would like to like them. Talking to yourself then starts to neutralize the every-day, all-day attack. You can talk yourself out of liking the creamy and sugary delights, and talk yourself into preferring more wholesome foods.

Sounds easy? It is. It takes a few minutes a day, certainly less time than exercising, medicating and visits to the doctor. It takes know-how, most of which you can get in this book. And it takes the willingness to try. This should come easiest of all to those who have gone through herculean efforts of diet, only to suffer the heartaches of seeing the weight gradually pile on again a few short weeks or months after the diet ended.

One young mother writes:

> I never had a serious weight problem until after the birth of my second child. At that time, I managed to take off about 25 pounds by dieting rigidly. There was no medication involved. I found it an extremely difficult task and only after five months did I eventually succeed. This happened ten years ago. About six years ago I started to gain weight again. No longer feeling that I could "do it myself," I resorted to the so-called diet pill. I lost weight rapidly and after eliminating the pills, I gained back twice as much. Off and on over the years, I kept going to different doctors and the same thing happened. My last attempt was about a year ago. At that time, I reacted very badly to the medication given me. My hands shook, my mind was foggy, and I had difficulty in expressing myself. I stopped. I weighed about 200 pounds at the time.
>
> In April of this year, I had reached 214 pounds. To say the least, I was depressed, uncomfortable and saw no hope for myself. At that time, a friend who had undergone hypnosis for smoking suggested that perhaps the hypnologist might help me. I decided to try it, though I really felt it was a lot of nonsense.

In the next two months, this person lost 26 pounds. Her weight loss continued effortlessly. She was soon down to a "happy" weight, and she has stayed there. Here is how she describes it:

> The process, my state of mind, the ease with which I diet all have the earmarks of a miracle.
>
> From the beginning, my choice of foods was correct. There was no premeditation or analysis of what I was eating. I seemed to want what I was supposed to eat. My meals were delicious and I had no cravings for cake, candy, ice cream, etc. I did at times crave food—cheese, grapefruit, meat! In all this time, I have never once felt I was dieting. I seem to gravitate toward the high protein foods, and I am enjoying them immensely!

For many years stars of Hollywood and Broadway have found talking themselves thin the easiest and most healthful way to doff poundage. Highly lucrative careers depend upon attractive, healthy bodies. Hypnosis and self-hypnosis have become much more common terms in these pace-setting circles.

How you can broadcast to yourself

Auto-conditioning is like broadcasting to yourself. It consists of three basic steps. First, in order to talk to your subconscious most effectively, you must divert the conscious mind so that it presents as little resistance as possible. This is usually done by assuming a quiet attitude, like the way you relax in your easy chair when you watch TV. Second, you must convince the subsconscious that what it thinks it likes, it should really dislike. This you do by actually talking to yourself—out loud or silently, through visualization. Finally, you must encourage the subconscious to like what your conscious intelligence knows to be beneficial. The readiness of the subconscious to obey implicitly is the secret of the success of this method.

Another built-in success factor is the progressive ease with which auto-conditioning is accomplished. Each time you relax and talk to yourself, it happens more quickly and more effectively. You can actually deepen your relaxation with practice to the point where it can be called a pleasant trance-like state. In this state your subconscious is practically naked to the spoken word, ready to do your intelligent bidding.

Part of that bidding can be to deepen the state even more the next time. The following session, without even trying, you will sink more quickly into an even deeper state of receptivity. As sure as the conditioned reflex, you will make even greater strides in molding your eating habits to be automatically perfect for you without strain, will power, or effort.

Self-hypnosis, or auto-conditioning, becomes easier and easier. First, you may induce relaxation by counting from one to ten. Later, you can count by two's—two, four, six, eight, ten—and reach the relaxed state in double-quick time. Finally, you will be able to command yourself to assume the relaxed state merely by thinking of the number ten.

How it works

The idea of talking to the subconscious can present a block to many people. Are you talking to some automaton, some robot, some entity other than yourself? The answer is no. Your subconscious is most definitely *you*. When you talk to your subconscious you are talking to *yourself*. (Italicized *you* and *yourself* will be used in the chapters ahead in place of the word "subconscious." You and yourself will be the person you, your family, and friends know you yourself to be. *You* and *yourself* will be the slave and master that remembers all, obeys implicitly, and controls you.)

You can talk to *yourself* right now. Say "I hate cake!" Say it either out loud or silently. Say it again. Now again. You have said it three times. Of course, you still like cake. But one thing is sure: you don't like it more than you did a minute ago, and very likely the next time you face up to cake, you will remember this moment.

If you were placed in a state of hypnosis and told three times that cake tastes as bad to you as some food for which you cherish a particular dislike, you would not be likely to eat cake again. The method of talking to *yourself* taught you in this book is a form of self-hypnosis better-known as auto-conditioning. Your success will depend a great deal on how closely you follow the relaxation techniques described in chapters ahead. Exposing your subconscious to your suggestion is the key.

Using imagery while the subconscious is exposed is the basic technique. What is imagery? You use it every day without being consciously aware of it. Try it now. Here is how you can practice. Get some white cards or small white sheets of scratch paper. Draw a circle in pencil. Hold it about one foot in front of your eyes. Stare at it. Now close your eyes. Try to picture it. Can you imagine how it looks?

Now draw a square. Close your eyes and picture it. Then put the square in the circle. Try to visualize that. Now without actually drawing the square's diagonals, close your eyes and visualize the square inside the circle with diagonal corners connected by crossing lines.

You will be using this power of imagining to picture yourself the attractive, slender person you are going to be. It will help you get there faster. Begin this imagining now by looking at your face in the mirror. Then close your eyes and try to see your face. Was your hair combed? Did a double chin show? Now picture your hair groomed just the way you want it. Picture the chin firm and youthful. Do this often and you will find yourself paying more attention to the hair. What about the chin? There will be some surprises there, too!

Refusing becomes easier than indulging

Properly receptive, your subconscious will respond automatically. You will eat with gusto just what you have instructed *yourself* to enjoy. You will turn away effortlessly from what you are not supposed to enjoy. You will be on a permanent diet without knowing it. You will be able to pass up pie a la mode and never feel deprived. You will eat fruit and gelatin desserts and savor them as much as baked alaska.

As the days go by, the scale will register increasing weight losses. You will be surprised every time you step on the scale. You have not dieted through painful self-discipline. Yet you will lose as much weight as if you had followed those type-written diet sheets religiously. Without the pain of deprivation, the days will add up to weeks faster and the weeks will fly by faster. Two pounds or more a week will soon register 10, 20, 30 pounds off on the scale!

There is no limit to the weight you can safely lose by talking yourself thin, as compared to other more difficult methods. Once you attain your normal weight, there's no diet to stop, no process to reverse. You stay thin—naturally. It's as simple as that!

Are you ready to try? And are *you* ready, too? Then, here goes!

REVIEW

Plan now to reserve a few minutes every day at a certain time to practice relaxation and auto-suggestion.

Start practicing visualization now, using the procedures on page 24.

2

WHY SELF-HYPNOSIS IS THE MOST EFFECTIVE REDUCING AGENT AVAILABLE

Talk yourself thin and you stay thin. You are not on another fad to trim fat. Auto-conditioning is the ultimate method to grow and stay slender because it changes the very mechanism that has motivated you to eat the fat-producing foods. It spells the end in your life of painful poundage and the beginning of new-found youth, health, and vigor.

However, it is not like a pill that can be downed with a gulp of water. To begin this method and follow it through takes conviction. You must know beyond a shadow of a doubt that:

1. No amount of pills, Turkish baths, exercising, starvation, or purgation will take pounds off *permanently*.
2. No overweight person can ever attain a full measure of health, happiness, and longevity.
3. Your subconscious motivates you to eat and can be instructed to motivate you to eat correctly.

These seem like simple enough truisms. Nothing to dispute here. But the subconscious has a way of playing tricks on us to protect its present ways. The subconscious can actually rationalize. You may wonder why you suddenly think there is no crime in being overweight; and, after all, are not pleasingly plump people a good-natured lot? Or you may find yourself misplacing this book repeatedly and wonder why. These are the tricks of the sub-conscious, striking back to protect its adopted ways.

So the first step is to reinforce your knowledge beyond a shadow of a doubt that diet pills can be dangerous; that steam rooms, massages, enemas and exercise are devices that deceive overweight people. The truth is that your real self is slender, attractive, popular, successful and happy; and that the method of auto-conditioning spelled out in this book is the easiest, quickest and most permanent way to attain your fullest potential.

This chapter, and the next, will help do this by reminding you of what you already know, so you can start the actual process of talking yourself thin on a soundly conditioned foundation, well able to ward off attempts by your subconscious to foil you.

Why self-hypnosis is growing in popularity

Today, more and more physicians and dentists are utilizing hypnosis in their practices. Now an accepted science, it has attained firm recognition from the medical profession. The successful use of hypnotism has been thoroughly documented in dental surgery, childbirth, neuroses, and obesity. Thousands of case histories attest to its successful use in eliminating unwanted habits such as excessive smoking, bed-wetting, alcoholism. In short, it is sure to be the preferred way to weight-loss among these very physicians now prescribing drugs to do the job. Dr. Frank S. Caprio and psychologist Joseph R. Berger say in their book *Helping Yourself with Self-Hypnosis:* [1]

---

[1] Frank S. Caprio, M.D. and Joseph R. Berger, *Helping Yourself with Self-Hypnosis* (Englewood Cliffs, N.J.: Prentice-Hall, Inc., 1963).

The authors, having engaged in a five-year research project with actual patients to see what hypnosis can do, concluded that since all hypnosis is self-hypnosis, the average person can be taught the techniques of self-hypnosis to increase his confidence, the zest for living and other real accomplishments of his choosing.

The authors point out that "self-suggestion is gaining greater recognition as a more desirable means of developing new lifelong sensible eating habits and maintaining weight control."

Sure, you can lose weight by exercise! Don't let anybody tell you that you can't. You can lose a pound a day, by walking ten hours a day. That's if you go at it briskly. If that sounds impractical, take a bicycle and you will only have to pedal seven hours for that pound. Swim and it will take only four hours—if the water is fairly cold. Ever hear of the calorie? It is a unit used to measure the heat or energy-producing content of foods. One pound of human fat is usually considered to be equivalent to about 3500 calories. Calories enter the body when we eat, are expended by the body in keeping warm and active.

How activity expends calories, and hence pounds, is illustrated in Table I. Obviously a fat man expends more calories walking than a thin man. It is more work. You must multiply the calorie factor by your weight to get your probable calorie consumption for a given exercise.

For instance, if you weigh 200 pounds and want to know the effects on your weight of a moderately fast two-hour walk, first multiply 200 by the calories per hour factor 1.9. This equals 380 calories per hour, or 760 calories in two hours. To translate this into pounds, divide by 3500. The weight lost by the two-hour hike would be .217 pounds.

One thing about exercise, it builds up the appetite. Of course, if you have an extra helping of steak and potatoes or an extra slice of pie, better hop back on the bicycle for

Table I

CALORIES CONSUMED BY ACTIVITY

	Calories per Hour per Pound (Multiply by Present weight)
Sleeping	0.4
Sitting	0.6
Standing	0.6
Walking slowly	1.3
Active exercise	1.8
Walking moderately fast	1.9
Severe exercise	2.8
Running	3.6
Very severe exercise	3.8
Running very fast	4.7

another few hours to even things out. There'll be a snack waiting for you in the refrigerator when you get back.

How about passive exercise? This is where you lie down and a masseur or machine moves you, pounds you or vibrates you. It is another dead end street in your search to lose weight. Your muscles may get denser, your body shape may improve, your dimensions may even diminish. But the needle on the scale won't budge.

Have you ever been on a diet? Chances are you weigh more today than the day you stopped dieting. For the day you stop marks the day you begin the return to your former weight, give or take a little.

Whether it is fat-free, protein-high, or carbohydrateless, a diet always works. Stick to it religiously and the pounds will drop away one by one. When you have had enough, watch your same old bulges ease themselves back into the same old places.

For some strange reason, the stronger your will-power during a diet, the more rapid is your return to self-indulgence later. It seems to follow the law of physics that says for every action there is an equal and opposite reaction. Psychologists speak of a law of reverse effect—the harder the unsure person tries, the greater the belief that he cannot succeed. Self-discipline, no matter what the area, carries within itself the seeds of its own destruction; and the more rugged that discipline is, the harder it falls.

Is dieting out? Not at all. But instead of you being the regulator, let *yourself* be the regulator. Subconscious control by *yourself* is effortless control. All you have to do is contact *yourself*, give *yourself* the proper, natural, healthful eating instructions, and the rest is automatic. You do not realize you are on a diet. In fact, it is not a diet, really. You eat the proper diet-prescribed foods and love them. You do not feel deprived when you refuse cake or ice cream. Instead, you feel deprived if you eat cake or ice cream and pass up fruit Jell-O or a fresh fruit compote.

How your subconscious can change your eating habits

Will your subconscious accept your new eating habits? You have enjoyed cake and ice cream, french fried potatoes, and pizza pies for a long, long time. How long will it take your subconscious to change its ways?

It can change instantly. If you can reach your deep subconscious and instruct it, it obeys from that moment on. However, it takes practice to reach the subsconscious in depth. Your first attempts at relaxation and the delivery of proper suggestions to your subconscious will have some results. But you will need to continue the procedure until your state of relaxation is so complete that the conscious self no longer stands between your suggestions and their target. Only then will the suggestion that "proteins are better for my body than carbohydrates" sink in. That thought becomes part of the automatic mechanism that makes you act the way you do. You will notice your outright eagerness to eat the right foods;

it will be the most normal thing in the world for you to do, just as if you have always been eating correctly.

In fact, your subconscious is so ready to obey you that you can pull the wool over its eyes if you want to. You can actually reverse the taste of two foods. For instance, suppose you despise the taste of spinach, but love spaghetti. You can actually convince your subconscious, through simple, repeated suggestion, that spinach tastes as good as spaghetti, and that spaghetti tastes just as horrible as spinach.

So not only is our subconscious amenable to reason, it is amenable to lack of reason, too. Unfortunately we are all exposed to plenty of the latter in our daily contacts with family, friends and the forces of salesmanship. Did you ever set off a chain of yawns by releasing a real sleepy one yourself? It is hard to watch somebody yawn and not be affected by the suggestion yourself.

How patterns of suggestibility work

During World War II, the liner Queen Mary left New York harbor one evening with a large contingent of the Women's Army Corps. The ship was outfitted as a troop carrier and was blacked out, as were all the ships in its convoy. In one cabin where 12 WAC's were bedded down in space usually occupied by two or three, several girls complained of the lack of ventilation. Finding it impossible to sleep, one of the girls felt her way to the blacked out porthole. As the girls waited literally breathlessly, she fumbled with the mechanism. Finally, she announced "I've got it!" All the girls breathed in the welcome relief and soon all were fast asleep. The next morning they discovered that the porthole was covered with an air-tight shield and never had been really opened. But the power of suggestion had done its good work.

Patterns of suggestibility can vary from the involuntary yawn to analgesia, or the inability to feel pain. The author can command his hand to go limp and to feel no pain. Before your eyes the blood will leave the hand and the fingers will droop like a wilted flower. You can then light a match and hold the flame in contact with the fingers. There will be no pain, and what is more astounding, no blister will form.

This demonstration is possible only because there have been repeated sessions of auto-suggestion in an extremely deep, almost trance-like state of relaxation. With each successive session, the subconscious is more totally controlled and primed for the next session, until a time is reached when merely the thought "now" is needed to produce the limp state. A word about that blister that did not form: it is possible to perform the reverse experiment on a hypnotized subject and suggest that a coin being placed on the body is red hot. In this case, the body dutifully creates a blister, though no heat has been applied.

Indian fakirs are famous for lying on beds of nails. Hawaiian kahunas are known to have walked on hot lava flows. Many tribal rituals throughout the primitive areas of the world include walking on hot coals without apparent pain or burns to the flesh. All of these are possible through self-hypnosis.

Medical science is learning how to use this technique in more and more ways to take the place of anesthesia and even to alter bodily functions. Hemorrhaging during an operation on a hypnotized patient has been commanded to stop, and it has stopped. Why? How? We do not know. It still is beyond the ability of scientists to agree on satisfactory explanations.

Fortunately, talking yourself thin involves no such complicated and dramatic goings on as these. You relax. You quiet yourself further. You deepen the state. You visualize your new way of wholesome eating. You evict bad habits arising from wrong suggestions. You plant proper suggestions in their place. You go about your business. You enjoy a new and better life.

How to demonstrate your own suggestibility

You know that auto-suggestion has been completely successful for others. But will it work for you? Are you as suggestible as others? The answer is yes, you are, no matter who you are, and you can prove it to yourself.

Cut a piece of string or thread about nine to ten inches long. Attach a small spherical button or bead at the end. Now take a piece of white unlined paper and draw on it a circle about two inches in diameter.

Read these instructions through first, then actually perform this test in quiet surroundings. Sit at a table. Rest your left arm comfortably on the table. Place your right elbow on the table and hold the end of the string in your hand with the wrist slightly forward. Place the paper under the pendulum you have made so that the center of the circle is directly under the sphere. Hold the string so that the pendulum just clears the paper. Loop the string over your finger for stability. Now adjust yourself so as to be very comfortable. If you are sitting properly, the pendulum should hang in front of the center of your body and the sphere or button should be about one half inch above the top of the table top.

Now sit very quietly and at ease. The pendulum is motionless. Visualize it beginning to move gently back and forth, left to right, right to left, left to right, right to left. Actually *will* it to move. See the pendulum actually swing in your mind's eye. Auto-suggestion is at work. The pendulum is swinging.

Put the book down on the table you will use. Read this pendulum test over, stopping at each paragraph to carry out the instructions.

Once you have demonstrated that you are indeed suggestible, you can heighten your suggestibility by visualizing the pendulum going in a circle. Now make it go around the other way by visualizing it reverse itself.

Why does the pendulum obey? Is this mind over matter? In a way. You are not consciously exerting any effort to swing the pendulum. But by visualizing the movement while you are in a relaxed state, you are influencing your subconscious to exert that effort and to perform the necessary manipulation of the hand. You are telling *yourself* to move the pendulum and *you* obey.

Like eating properly, this auto-suggested performance took no actual will-power other than the will to relax and visualize. The rest came unconsciously, easily, effortlessly.

Here's another test. It is done with an imaginary shopping bag. Read this paragraph through, then put the book down and try it. Sit in a straight-backed chair. Hold your arms out horizontally in front of you. Now close your eyes and visualize someone's placing over your weaker wrist the handle of a loaded shopping bag. It is very heavy. Your arm is tiring, lowering. Repeat this to yourself for about a minute while you visualize the bag. At this point open your eyes, and see for yourself.

Another test of suggestibility is performed in the standing position. Turn your back to a clear wall and stand erect about two inches from it. Read the rest of this paragraph, then put the book down and test yourself. Look up toward the ceiling. Close your eyes. Imagine that the wall has suddenly acquired a magnetic force that unmistakably draws you to it. As you count to 10 it gets stronger, pulling irresistibly on the small of your back. You are drawn to touch the wall.

Suggestibility actually needs no test. We have it as sure as we breathe. We see it in the ball park where people yell together and in theatres where they applaud together. It is the motivation behind crowd behavior everywhere. We see it at the check-out counters in every supermarket where Mr. and Mrs. Consumer have unknowingly responded to such subtle persuaders as color, packaging, shelf height, and brand name.

The person with rose fever may sneeze at the sight of plastic, imitation roses. The child who has been warned that he will get a cold in a draft, can develop a running nose just by passing an open window. The woman who believes she became pregnant can develop all the symptoms of pregnancy.

The problem is not whether or not we are suggestible. Rather, it is how can we most beneficially utilize our suggestibility.

Why imagination is more powerful than will power

The way to harness your suggestibility, is to know what to say to *yourself* and how to say it. Talking yourself thin can be done without actually uttering an audible word. People talk to themselves all the time. In some rare cases they startle you by talking out loud. Even those who mumble or move their lips are stand-outs enough to make you wonder. Most of us talk to ourselves silently, with thoughts that are either in word form or image form. In either case it is our imagination that is utilized.

The power of the imagination is the greatest power on earth. Every accomplishment in this material world has first been imagined. It is the step before the written word, design, or blueprint. There is even evidence that what we do not want, but hold in the imagination through fear, comes.

In the body, imagination sets off stimuli. Imagine a sizzling steak and the saliva begins to flow. You could not set off your saliva by sheer will-power no matter how hard you tried. It is imagination that causes impotence, fear of water, and a multitude of emotional disorders. Harnessed to motivate in a positive direction, imagination can work miracles in health, and well-being.

Talking to *yourself* is an exercise in imagining. You put your imagination through the proper paces then you learn how to develop it and train it. You permit it to work closely with your subconscious, unobstructed by your conscious thoughts. As a team they are unconquerable.

Look at the uselessness of will-power in drug addiction, gambling, alcoholism. You have your own experience to prove the uselessness of will-power in weight control. To abandon useless will-power and to embrace useful imagination power is to insure permanent success in self-mastery.

Using the "as if" principal

Ever since Emile Coué, the French psychologist, had people looking into the mirror and saying "Day by day in every way, I am feeling better and better," there have been many books, treatises and correspondence courses on how to use imagery and auto-suggestion to your advantage. One reason why they had only superficially good results is that they failed to convince the reader or student that unequivocal acceptance is essential.

The degree to which auto-suggestion will help you is dependent on how you will apply the "As If" principal.

This "As If" principle states that you have to accept suggestions you give yourself "as if" they were true. The man with rose fever does not sneeze if he knows that the flowers are artificial. He sneezes because he knows they are real, even though they are not. It is *as if* they were. The child's nose begins to run when he walks by an open window because he knows he will get a cold being in a draft. It is *as if* it were true.

Of course, you will be giving yourself true suggestions. But if you think they won't work, they won't. If you know they will work, they will. If you accept your own suggestions as if they are already an accomplished fact, accomplished they will be.

This book will take you through the necessary training exercises to influence your logical faculty to put its trust in you. You will know yourself to be an important authority about yourself. You will be impressed consciously as well as subconsciously in whatever you have to say to or about yourself. You will become a very important person to yourself and to *yourself*. You will have an uncritical acceptance of everything you have to say in the fascinating conversation that is about to unfold.

How habit reinforces suggestion

The nice thing about all of this is that it is easy to start and even easier to progress. It's like power steering in your car. A built-in mechanism assists you whichever way you turn. In fact, it's better than power steering. As you use it, it becomes still easier and easier.

In the first one or two tries at the auto-suggestion exercise, you can include the suggestion that you will enjoy doing the exercise again soon. And you will, truly. You don't have to do this very often because soon habit takes over. It reinforces suggestion and keeps the new process rolling almost automatically.

Habit does this; you know it does. You have seen habit at work against proper eating. You ate improperly, automatically, and loved it. Now, with habit working for you, you will eat properly, automatically, and love it just as much.

In this chapter you have reminded yourself of what you already know. Reducing pills are a dead end street, and all other methods merely tilt the scales temporarily. You have become acquainted with what perhaps you did not know— that with very little more effort than it takes to read this book, you can actually talk yourself thin.

If you have any doubts at all about the dangers of remaining overweight; if you find yourself thinking that "I have a big frame," or "Overweight is hereditary in my family," or "My problem is glandular and I'll never be able to do anything about it"; if you are thinking any nice things at all about those fat bulges, chances are your subconscious is starting to defend its present ways. This is its way of hitting back. It is "custard's" last stand. Better hurry on to Chapter 3.

REVIEW

Practice the pendulum test for suggestibility on page 34. Also practice the shopping bag test for suggestibility on page 35. Both tests will serve to heighten your ability to visualize and prepare you for talking the language your habit-forming subconscious understands.

3

HOW TO TAKE
YOUR FIRST POSITIVE STEP
TOWARD THE NEW YOU

This is a how-to-do-it book. It is a step-by-step instruction manual that will enable you to carry out normal goals of weight loss through self-hypnotism. You will find it an easy book to use. But so is a dictionary. Yet the average person does not know how to make fullest use of a dictionary. Either he has forgotten, or he has never read the introductory pages that tell the key to pronunciation, syllabication, compounding, preferential use, and so on.

This chapter will tell you how to use this book. It will tell you where to stop reading and start talking to yourself and when to start reading again. It will guide you along the way to skillfully inducing a deep state of relaxation. It will instruct you on the proper management of that state for the most healthful benefits through the subconscious. It will describe in detail the process of terminating that state so as to place you on a higher and higher level of vibrant enthusiasm and radiant spirits.

Exactly when does one put the book down and start following instructions? Can you terminate a state of relaxation in order to read on a few more paragraphs and see what comes next? These questions are answered for you. The book, in effect, takes you by the hand all the way.

How to use "stop and go" reading

All it takes is one reading of this book to make you relatively skillful in the ways of auto-suggestion. In fact, half way through the book you will be practicing those skills and already changing your eating habits. That practice is essential. By actually doing the relaxation exercises and going through the mental exercises you are beginning the process of weight loss.

You cannot read a do-it-yourself book on building a boat or hi-fidelity equipment as you would a novel, and expect to find the boat or hi-fi waiting for you when you finish. It takes stop and go reading. When you stop, the project goes. Your weight control project will go better and better as each chapter provides you with keys to improving different phases of the talk-yourself-thin process.

Every chapter will close with a review of exactly what you should practice before starting the next chapter. If you are reading in the evening, practice in bed before falling asleep and again on rising. You are then ready to start the next chapter. Actually, you can practice anytime, anywhere, even in the subway on your way to work. Practicing auto-suggestion brings swift results. No long sessions are required. Your memory mechanism is in sharper focus than it has ever been. In fact, many scholars are now using auto-suggestion to improve their memory power. The suggestions that you give *yourself* are never forgotten by the subconscious.

Tailor your attitude

Some years ago, a great Negro comedian decided to find out if his act was really funny or if people were laughing because of his reputation as a comedian. He entered an amateur show after explaining his reasons to the manager. He put on the pantomine act that had made him famous. In a few minutes the audience was cat-calling and jeering. Out came the "hook" and he was pulled off the stage. Then the manager came out and explained who the comedian was. He came back on stage to thunderous applause, repeated the same act and the audience nearly tore the house down.

Nothing changed in this episode, except the audience's attitude. In the first instance the attitude was one of inferiority, misery and failure associated with most amateurs. In the latter instance, the attitude was one of strength, accomplishment and success associated with stars. Identical circumstances, approached with opposite attitudes, bring about widely different results.

If you approached auto-suggestion with the same sense of despair and futility that you might approach another diet, you would be working against yourself. On the other hand, if you approach this new method confident that you will succeed as others have, you are a giant step closer to that success.

It is essential that you disregard past failures. This is the time—right now—to tear up old score cards and start fresh. Your motivation and interest should be at a peak; your expectations, the greatest. You must be confident that you are on the threshold of a new life of self-mastery.

As you acquire more healthful eating habits, it will be more by substitution than elimination. You will be enjoying proper foods with the same gusto that you now enjoy starchy foods. Chances are there will be no major change in the sum total of your eating activity and therefore little risk of a new habit moving in as an outlet for some emotional need.

This is less true for those that are grossly overweight than it is for those that need to shed 5 to 50 pounds. If your overweight problem is severe, with excess poundage exceeding 30% of your proper weight, you may not be able to discover your emotional need. Seriously overweight persons sometimes have serious, deep-set emotional or organic problems. For those persons, auto-suggestive methods will succeed in bringing about weight loss, but the causation may persist unless treated psychiatrically or medically. By far the majority of the millions of overweight people weigh too much because they eat too much of the wrong foods. In any case it is a wise precaution to let your family physician examine you as you talk yourself thin.

How to use visualization

In a way you have already started to talk yourself thin. In Chapter 1 you visualized yourself thin. In Chapter 2 you demonstrated your suggestibility by talking *yourself* into moving the pendulum. Granted, this is only a first "hello," but it is an important beginning. It would do right now to resolve to practice the pendulum exercise right after this stretch of reading, and also to visualize yourself thin every time you look in the mirror.

In the case of the pendulum, make it move in straight lines left to right, then right to left. Then in circles, first one way then the other. Do it by visually imagining it moving just as you want it to move, and watch it go as your subconscious obeys. This will give you more practice in using the imagination during the your conversations with *yourself*. Later, in a relaxed state, the power of imagery will be easier for you to use and more effective, too, than the spoken word. You will be visualizing "stop" foods as wrong for you and "go" foods as right for you. By that time there will be plenty of starch in the conversation and pendulums will be forgotten, as pancakes, potatoes, and pop-overs become frequent topics of self-discussion.

When you look in the mirror, slowly turn away from what you see. Now close your eyes and visualize a thinner face, less chin. Now extend the view to full length. First the front view, then side views, each time removing bulges at the hips, stomach, etc. in your imagination. Repeat this exercise as a regular procedure every time you glimpse yourself in a mirror. And if you can do it in between times as well, it will mean more power to you.

Action steps like these will develop with increasing frequency as you read on. Why not underline them or tab them in some way so that they stand out for quick review and practice as you move along.

Begin your progress chart

As you read this book and follow the instructions you will begin to lose weight. A visual record of your weight changes will be useful to you. It will act as a progress chart, giving you a goal, and alerting you when you level off.

Here is how to make the chart. Use a piece of standard cross-section (graph) paper, or line a plain piece of white paper, standard 8½ x 11 inch size. There should be eight to ten lines to the inch. Paste it on a piece of cardboard. Now, with the long axis of the paper vertical draw a horizontal line near the bottom 60 squares long. These are days. Label them as such and mark them off from left to right in fives along the bottom starting with today's date. At the left of the page draw a vertical line joining with the end of the horizontal line and extending up about 80 squares. Each of these is one half pound. Place your present weight at the top. Mark off the squares at the left, decreasing one pound every two squares. (Your progress chart should now look something like that on page 46.)

Put a dot at your weight on the left hand line. Tomorrow place a dot at your weight on the next square to the right and connect the two dots. Do the same each day. Naturally your weight graph will not start to descend noticeably until you are well along in this book. Then, watch it drop!

How fast and how much? Weight losers will want to set a goal for themselves. A good safe rule of thumb is 1% of your weight per week. If you weigh 150 pounds, your goal would

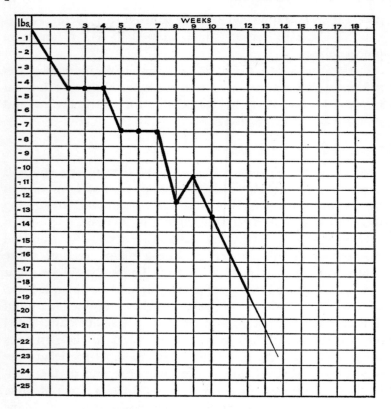

Weight Loss Progress Chart

be 1.5 pounds lost each week. At the end of your chart, eight and a half weeks away, your goal would call for a loss of about 13 pounds, down to 137. Figure out a goal for yourself. Draw a dotted line on your chart, starting a few days from now and running down to the mark you have set for yourself eight and a half weeks hence.

When you enter your weight on your progress chart and graph its descent, chances are it will drop faster the first and second weeks, flattening out somewhat after that. It will even level off completely at some point. However, auto-suggestions will be given to you in later chapters that will send your weight tumbling again.

The art of relaxation

Developing your ability to relax will be an important part of the instruction that lies ahead. You can develop the art into a science, one that will stand you in good stead no matter who you are or what you do. Executives in every walk of life are learning that a few minutes of quiet relaxation brings hours of surging energy.

Use this book to master a technique of relaxation if you use it for nothing else. Banish tension and you rid yourself of one of the major causes of physical breakdown and disease. Acquire the skill to relax at will and you can look years younger and feel more alive. A few minutes of deep relaxation is a combination beauty treatment, pick-me-up, and tonic.

Select the method that suits you best. Read the words that are recommended, but do not feel obligated to memorize them. Rather, understand their purpose and say it in your own way. When the text suggests that you put the book down and try it, that is a good time to stop, while the understanding of the purpose is fresh. Resist the impulse to read on and see what comes next, or else you will finish the book and your progress chart will read "no change."

Use either the sensory or the motor method

There are two popular methods of relaxation, the sensory method and the motor method. With the sensory method you use the imagination to picture yourself in a setting of peace, beauty and tranquility—like a lazy beach in Hawaii. With the motor method you use the imagination to picture yourself in a state of muscular immobility—heavy, rigid, lethargic.

Relaxation by either method is enjoyable. Decide to have

fun at it by the method that comes easiest to you. You will
find you attain a blissful state by either method. It is in this
state that suggestions which you speak or think to *yourself*
have a profound effect. And yet you are not asleep. You are
possibly a little drowsy. You won't feel like being bothered,
but you are awake and aware of all that goes on. If the doorbell or telephone rings, you will hear it. If water boils over
on the stove you will be able to rise to the domestic crisis just
as quickly and efficiently as if it had happened while you
were working or reading. There is no reason to fear a deep
state of relaxation as a trance, or semi-consciousness. It is
none of these. And yet it permits impressions to be made
on the subconscious as if it were both of these. Deepening
the relaxation does not lessen your awareness. It does heighten
your suggestibility and induce a greater, uncritical acceptance of your suggestions, while you pay less attention to outside sounds.

Some who first attempt to relax by these methods may actually doze off. This happens with release of tension. When you
learn the next step—that of talking to *yourself* in the relaxed
state—this slight activity will keep you awake.

If you are fortunate enough to own a tape recorder, you
can combine the advantages of recorded repetition with those
of conscious imagery. When you are given the phrases in future chapters to induce relaxation or other conversation elements to talk yourself thin, record them using your own
voice. Listening to the repeated suggestions coming from
your own voice while you are in the state of deep relaxation
can be very effective.

How to categorize your food

The suggestions that you use to talk yourself thin will be
aimed at encouraging your attraction to healthful, nourishing
foods and discouraging your attraction to rich, fattening
foods. But before you can dish out these suggestions, you

must know one from the other. To help simplify identification, "go" foods and "stop" foods will be listed. Carbohydrate content tables will help to show why these foods are friend or foe.

Some foods are hard to categorize. They contain too much carbohydrate for really conscientious reducing, but too little to interfere with mild weight-losing schedules. These will be placed in a "caution" list from which you may choose according to your own goals. If you permit yourself a number of "caution" foods, there may come a time when your progress chart flattens out and *you* don't. This will be the signal for you to transfer these from "caution" to "stop" foods.

On the other hand, when your weight approaches normal and you no longer wish to lose, you may re-introduce foods on the "caution" list and, through suggestion, make them once more part of your new eating pattern. You will never want to reintroduce "stop" foods. These are the common every day culprits that are banished from your new normality. Their return would spell weight return. Without them, you are permanently thin, you miss them not, and you could not care less that they exist.

If you sneak a peek at the list now, you would not feel that way. Instead, you will see the most tantalizing, mouth-watering dishes on the "stop" list—most of the delicious desserts you have grown to love. Grown and grown and grown.

Look at that same list after a few sessions of talking to *yourself* and you will wonder how you could ever have eaten that sickening mush. The lusty, savory "go" foods will become doubly and triply attractive.

Your physician can be helpful in selecting "go" and "stop" foods for you. He is especially important in such decisions if you already suffer from some of the obesity ailments previously described, or in fact, from any chronic ailment.

Your own voluntary choice of "go" foods and your decision to put a stop to "stop" foods is in no way embarking on a diet, any more than you are on a diet now. You have been brain-washed and sweet-tasted into an attraction for starchy, sugary foods. You are now neutralizing the magnet and remagnetiz-ing it into attracting other, more wholesome, foods in the same way. Basically you will be eliminating excess carbohy-drates from your eating pattern. There will still be all the carbohydrates your body needs in the "go" foods and more than your body needs in the "caution" foods. So it is not a diet, in the sense that it has to be prescribed for you. You are entirely free to eat the foods you want. It is just that soon you will not want these others.

Checklist of precautions

Persons suffering from an illness would see their physician anyhow, especially about eating habits. Advising them to do so now is about as valuable and original counsel as telling them to look both ways before crossing the street.

However, it cannot be left unsaid. And there are other precautions—common sense all, which nevertheless cannot be left unsaid.

This book, of course, should not be used by ill persons—mentally or physically ill.

Nor should this book be used by children. Adolescents may use it with adult supervision. Other "shake-well-before-us-ing" precautions might be:

"Don't give yourself an overdose." That is, don't set unrealis-tic or dangerous goals. Follow recommended goals even though it may take a few weeks longer. You will be thin a long, long time.

"Don't use contrary to directions." That is don't give your-self unwise suggestions, like ones that would destroy hun-ger or inhibit eating *per se*. That would be like swallowing iodine despite the label "Poison."

"If symptoms persist, see your doctor." That is if the compulsion to eat the foods is so strong that your suggestions are ineffective or they set up a conflict, chances are your unconscious motivations are deeply rooted in an existing neurosis. It is this neurosis that needs to be treated, by a psychiatrist or psychologist, rather than your eating habits.

Actually this book is good medicine, probably the best health-improver you have ever experienced. Forced down somebody's throat against their will, it would spell trespass, struggle, trouble. Read and used in a sincere desire to be your true, physically-fit slender self, it spells a joyous experience, an easy way to stay thin, and the end to trouble.

REVIEW

Practice the art of visualizing yourself thin. Every time you do this you pave the way for speedy and effective results to your auto-conditioning. Paste your progress chart on a piece of cardboard and mount it on the wall near your scale.

4

HOW YOUR WEIGHT
CAN MAKE YOU
SICK OR WELL

You are unhappy when overweight, whether or not you show it to your friends and family. You are not at peak health and vigor, even though you may not now suffer from any particular ailment. If you are 20% overweight or more (see Table II) you are among the more than 30 million people in the United States who are classified dangerously overweight. These people are prone to organic heart disease, diabetes mellitus, and gall stones. Their case histories read like a medical encyclopedia.

Two-thirds of these over-large folks are over forty. Padded in the rear or in the front, their troubles can be behind them, ahead of them, or both. Insurance companies put up with them only at a premium sufficiently increased so as to make up for the shorter time they will be around to pay them.

Even if you are only 10% overweight you are in trouble. True, only about half the trouble, but trouble. That's just enough to put a female out of style, provide the male with a tell-tale paunch, and give both male and female a noticeable social impedance. More significantly, the moderate bulges are shadows of bigger things to come.

Little wonder that so many people have been on the path to losing weight. What a pity their path is usually a treadmill.

TABLE II—AVERAGE WEIGHTS FOR MEN AND WOMEN
According to Height and Age

Height (In Shoes)*	Weight in Pounds (In Indoor Clothing)					
	Ages 20-24	Ages 25-29	Ages 30-39	Ages 40-49	Ages 50-59	Ages 60-69
Men						
5' 2"	128	134	137	140	142	139
3"	132	138	141	144	145	142
4"	136	141	145	148	149	146
5"	139	144	149	152	153	150
6"	142	148	153	156	157	154
7"	145	151	157	161	162	159
8"	149	155	161	165	166	163
9"	153	159	165	169	170	168
10"	157	163	170	174	175	173
11"	161	167	174	178	180	178
6' 0"	166	172	179	183	185	183
1"	170	177	183	187	189	188
2"	174	182	188	192	194	193
3"	178	186	193	197	199	198
4"	181	190	199	203	205	204
Women						
4'10"	102	107	115	122	125	127
11"	105	110	117	124	127	129
5' 0"	108	113	120	127	130	131
1"	112	116	123	130	133	134
2"	115	119	126	133	136	137
3"	118	122	129	136	140	141
4"	121	125	132	140	144	145
5"	125	129	135	143	148	149
6"	129	133	139	147	152	153
7"	132	136	142	151	156	157
8"	136	140	146	155	160	161
9"	140	144	150	159	164	165
10"	144	148	154	164	169	**
11"	149	153	159	169	174	**
6' 0"	154	158	164	174	180	**

* 1-inch heels for men and 2-inch heels for women.
** Average weights not determined because of insufficient data.
Note: Prepared by the Metropolitan Life Insurance Company.
Derived primarily from data of the Build and Blood
Pressure Study, 1959, Society of Actuaries.

TABLE III — DESIRABLE WEIGHTS FOR MEN AND WOMEN

According to Height and Frame. Ages 25 and Over

Height (In Shoes)*	Weight in Pounds (In Indoor Clothing)		
	Small Frame	Medium Frame	Large Frame
Men			
5' 2"	112–120	118–129	126–141
3"	115–123	121–133	129–144
4"	118–126	124–136	132–148
5"	121–129	127–139	135–152
6"	124–133	130–143	138–156
7"	128–137	134–147	142–161
8"	132–141	138–152	147–166
9"	136–145	142–156	151–170
10"	140–150	146–160	155–174
11"	144–154	150–165	159–179
6' 0"	148–158	154–170	164–184
1"	152–162	158–175	168–189
2"	156–167	162–180	173–194
3"	160–171	167–185	178–199
4"	164–175	172–190	182–204
Women			
4'10"	92– 98	96–107	104–119
11"	94–101	98–110	106–122
5' 0"	96–104	101–113	109–125
1"	99–107	104–116	112–128
2"	102–110	107–119	115–131
3"	105–113	110–122	118–134
4"	108–116	113–126	121–138
5"	111–119	116–130	125–142
6"	114–123	120–135	129–146
7"	118–127	124–139	133–150
8"	122–131	128–143	137–154
9"	126–135	132–147	141–158
10"	130–140	136–151	145–163
11"	134–144	140–155	149–168
6' 0"	138–148	144–159	153–173

* 1-inch heels for men and 2-inch heels for women.
Source: <u>Build and Blood Pressure Study, 1959,</u> Society of Actuaries.

This should not come as news to anyone. Walkers, dieters, vibrators and pill-takers need no reminder that theirs is a one-step forward two-steps back affair.

How much weight is over-weight

A study of insured persons was made in 1885-1900 and again in the period 1909-27. They resulted in age, height, weight tables that have remained in use for many years. However, in 1959, a study by the Society of Actuaries showed that some changes had occurred. Women became thinner. They weighed five to six pounds less than their turn of the century predecessors at the age of 25. Among men, on the other hand, there was an increase of five pounds, especially for short men. These new studies also confirmed that the lowest mortality generally occurs among the underweight.

The average weights for men and women, based on these 1959 studies, are shown in Table II. Desirable weights for men and women 25 and over are shown in Table III. This latter table divides people into those with small, medium and large frames. Obviously, a Fred Astaire the same height as a Winston Churchill would not have the same desirable weight. Nor should an Audrey Hepburn weigh the same as a Sophie Tucker.

Note that in both tables, height is measured with shoes on —1-inch heels for men, 2-inch heels for women. In Table II the weight includes usual indoor clothing.

Why you overeat

Over 50 years ago a group of overweight women formed TOPS, Take Off Pounds Sensibly. They met once a week to discuss why they overate. Today there are chapters all over the country. They provide the next best thing to psychological group therapy. By talking it out, these women discover they indulge themselves with between-meal meals and fattening snacks because of boredom, insecurity or a variety of other emotional reasons. With the realization of a cause for over-weight, comes the beginning of the cure.

After TOPS, came Alcoholics Anonymous founded on the same theory. Now there are also murmurings of Tobacco Anonymous and Neurotics Anonymous. Whether you talk to a group of people with a common problem, to your family physician, or to a psychologist or a psychiatrist, you will in time betray to them and to yourself the basic emotional cause of your overeating.

I have no emotional cause, you may say, I just get hungry. Sure you do. But if you are a young married woman, having to get used to all that time between the 8:00 A.M. farewell kiss and the 6:00 P.M. hello kiss, chances are you are going to en-joy an 11:00 A.M. snack and a 3:00 P.M. tea as a welcome interlude. The urge to enjoy these interludes is soon synony-mous with hunger.

If you are an up-and-coming salesman, there's nothing like talking to a customer over coffee, or lunch, or cocktails, or dinner. It clouds your cold-blooded sales pitch in an atmos-phere of warm cordiality. Soon a table in front of you with food on it becomes synonymous with income and wealth. Your stomach begins to send out hunger symptoms even after meals.

The causes of overeating are as diversified as the problems of life. They range from money to mothers-in-law, from sex to security. Part of the process of talking yourself thin will involve the kind of heart-to-heart discussion that can lead to at least a glimmering of understanding of why you happen to be a pushover for the carbohydrate bombardment. You may already suspect what that emotion is. On the other hand, it may be secreted below the conscious level. Talking yourself thin can be a two-way conversation and there are techniques for inducing your subconscious to come up with the answer.

Why do you need the answer if the subconscious will obey your eating instructions like a slave? Because it will help to prevent your taking on some other habit or indulgence to satisfy the want. Let us say you begin to realize that loneliness and boredom are the basic reasons behind your putting on the snack bag. And let us say you talk to *yourself* and successfully instruct your subconscious to eat less often and properly. At this point you may take on some unwanted habit. You may find that you become an incessant gumchewer, or you may take up smoking, or double your present smoking—all for the sake of that same loneliness and boredom.

On the other hand, if you begin to understand that your overeating is a result of some emotion stemming from your present environment, you may be able to substitute something of value for the food. The cigarettes or the gumchewing will have no room to move in when the over-eating moves out, if you make friends, hobbies, social work or other activities your answer to boredom. A spiritual or philosophical understanding of the nature of man and the universe may become the answer to insecurity.

Discovering the cause and prescribing the cure will be part of the adventure in the chapters ahead. Self-hypnosis will play an important role.

What overeating does to your body

To the camel, fat is protection against the lean, hungry desert days ahead. He stores it on his back. To man, fat is a sign of the rich, sugary dessert days past. No matter where he stores it, it is not a protection. It is a warning. It warns of emotional imbalance, diet imbalance, or both. And imbalance leads to a fall.

A rule of thumb popular with the insurance fraternity says that a person who is 50 years of age and 50 pounds overweight has a 50% less life expectancy. For a man of 50, this means a probability of nine years more of life instead of 18. For a woman of 50, it means a likelihood of ten more years to go, instead of 20.

No matter how old you are, a prolonged state of overweight will exact its toll. That damage to your health will be in proportion to your age, to the amount you are overweight, and to the length of time you are overweight. It behooves you to act while you have your youth, to act before you get too far out of hand, and to act as soon as possible.

The high death rate for overweight persons is largely a result of cardiovascular and renal diseases. These are diseases of the heart, blood vessels and kidneys.

But there is no limit to the kind of troubles your body can run into when it is struggling against fat. Chronic illness can become a way of life. It can begin with overtiredness and persistent fatigue. It can be reflected in aches, pains and swellings in your joints. It can bring malfunctioning of the digestive system.

Is your subconscious sending up thoughts of rebellion? "I guess I'll stop reading for a while." "I think I'll skip this part." Better keep reading. Remember, you need to be thoroughly aware of the dangers of obesity in order to ward off later just such tactics of the subconscious. Watch for it. You'll be hearing. "Well, I'm not *that* much overweight." "Maybe on me it looks good."

In medical terms, here is what is on tomorrow's menu for the seriously overweight. Arthritis is a favorite. In prolonged, gnawing un-relievable pain it probably exceeds many fold all the oral pleasure we had in becoming eligible. Then there is diabetes, a metabolic disorder in which the ability to oxidize carbohydrates is lost to a degree. It occurs when the pancreas fails to produce enough of the hormone insulin essential for the metabolism of carbohydrates. Symptoms are thirst, sugar in the urine, hunger, weakness and, in advanced cases, coma.

If this does not sound very appetizing, look further. The menu is a varied one. There is inflammation of the gall bladder, cirrhosis of the liver, and a variety of hernias. That item coronary thrombosis, means heart disease. There is also kidney disease. You can have varicose veins, arteriosclerosis, or just plain high blood pressure.

Overweight people make poor surgical patients. An overweight person who is operated on for appendicitis or gall bladder disease is a fatality four times as often as a normal weight person undergoing the identical operation.

Overweight people are also prone to accidents. This is a normal result of their lessened agility, slower reflexes, and sluggishness. They are also apt to find it more difficult to have children. Fertility and virility go down as weight goes up. If they do conceive, overweight women are likely to be in for complications during pregnancy, and a greater chance of a stillborn child.

The immortal mortality tables

Had enough? All right, but just top the whole mess off with a look at the two tables which follow:

Table IV–A

EXPECTATION OF LIFE AT VARIOUS AGES IN THE
UNITED STATES 1960 *

(Years)

| Age | White | | Nonwhite | | All |
	Male	Female	Male	Female	Races
0	67.4	74.1	61.1	66.3	69.7
20	50.1	56.2	45.5	49.9	52.4
40	31.6	37.1	28.4	32.1	33.8
45	27.2	32.5	24.6	28.0	29.4
50	23.1	28.0	21.0	24.3	25.2
55	19.3	23.8	17.8	20.9	21.3
60	15.9	19.7	14.9	17.7	17.6
65	12.9	15.9	12.7	15.2	14.3
70	10.2	12.4	10.7	12.7	11.3

* 1963 *Life Insurance Fact Book* (Institute of Life Insurance, 488 Madison Ave., New York, N.Y., 10022).

Table IV–B
YEARS LOST BY BEING OVERWEIGHT

Age	60% Overweight	25–60% Overweight	Up to 25% Overweight
		Years off life expectancy **	
		MEN	
35	28	20	12
40	30	20	11
45	21	19	14
50	18	16	13
55	12	10	8
60	11	10	8
65	9	8	7
70	8	7	5
		WOMEN	
35	23	15	7
40	22	15	7
45	22	15	7
50	20	14	6
55	16	12	5
60	13	9	4
65	10	7	3
70	9	7	3

** When excess weight has persisted some years.

These have not been prepared as a medical theory. They are the facts of life, and death, and derived from actual death certificates sampled throughout the country and borne out every year with very little deviation. The billion dollar insurance industry depends on them in setting premiums so that those premiums and the dividends thereon will be at least large enough to pay the face amount of the insurance on death.

In Table IV–B you can see how a woman, aged 35, who has

been up to 25% overweight for a number of years loses seven years off her life expectancy. Her male counterpart would be cheating himself of 12 years.

If you are more than 25% overweight, these years of life you may expect to lose can double.

Just look how sweet, sweet life is shortened by too many sweets—the ironic justice of it all.

Your right weight

By now you must be anxious to know what your right weight should be. It is the first step in building an image of the real, vital you which you will soon be on the way to attaining—easily and permanently.

You can see weight tables on just about every "Weigh Yourself" for a penny scale. They have been prepared by many sources. All of them are based on theory, or on the weight and measurement of a limited number of selected physical specimens. They usually relate your proper weight to your present height. And, of course, it is done separately for men and for women. One man, obviously not ready to believe what the table told him, as he stepped up and deposited his penny in a side-walk scale exclaimed, "My God, I'm three inches too short!"

Some of these tables make allowances for large, medium and small frames, a concession to the Winston Churchill-types among men and the Sophie Tucker among women. Bone structures do differ. Large frames weigh more and take more tissue and muscle to keep skin and bones together. But it is doubtful that we are talking about a swing of more than 5% in one direction or another.

Look up your weight in Table II. Use your erect height for this purpose. For this is your true height. Even though the burdens of the world and of your own weight are bending you low, it won't be ever thus. Once you attain your proper weight, your whole revitalized outlook will bring about a more erect posture. You may now add or subtract up to 5% depending on whether you feel you have a slender or stocky frame.

Remember your correct weight. You have seen it before, thought about it for a moment, and then dropped it. This time hang on to it. Say it aloud a few times. "My healthful and proper weight is —— pounds." Write it in that space. Look at the numerals you have written. Visualize yourself at that weight. Put the book down and think about that weight as you relax and prepare to read on.

Now you can have vim, vigor, vitality

You have just taken a very important step. You have used the power of your mind to set in motion the creative forces that will bring about exactly what you have visualized. Thought triggers the subconscious mind to get busy and work its magic. Suggestion, either our own or from the outside, has put our subconscious to work impelling us to eat our way to overweight. Now, suggestion, either our own or that of a qualified hypnologist, can reverse the procedure and make us thin.

It will change us in other ways, too. Some of these changes will be byproducts of the thinning process. Others will be set off directly by the switch to positive, constructive suggestions. Visualizing your correct weight is one of these suggestions. Picturing yourself erect, youthful and healthy can be other positive suggestions.

We live in a world where the positive dominates over the negative, where creation takes place faster than decay. Were it any different, there would have been no universe as we know it. Your positive thoughts—whether directed at making you thin or successful or healthy—given an equal time will prevail over your negative thoughts. You will be amazed at the power of these suggestions once you learn how to give them to yourself effectively.

Furthermore, you can pyramid the results by including in your positive suggestions to yourself the constructive thought that you will be talking to *yourself* more earnestly, more believably, and more frequently in the days ahead. The technique for doing this will be covered in detail in later chapters. But now is a good time to start picturing yourself thin, and full of the vim, vigor and vitality that comes with a slim figure or well-proportioned physique.

"I lost 60 pounds of failure"

There is so much case-history evidence pointing to increased success and happiness when an overweight person returns to normal that one wonders why obesity has ever been able to gain a body-hold in our society. More convincing than the dramatic success stories are the stories of the average Mary or Joe. Take for instance, Miss A, aged 36 and a school teacher. She taught special classes for emotionally disturbed children. She had been gradually gaining weight over ten years of on-and-off dieting. Now she weighed 230 and was suffering from ulcers.

She tried diet pills, but the ulcers interfered. She was hospitalized and put on a bland diet of milk and cream. Her weight rose to 250. She sank into fits of depression and anxiety. Periods of tiredness became more frequent until they merged and she became in a state of perpetual fatigue. Her work suffered and it became just a question of time how long she could continue at it.

It was then that another teacher told of her experience with weight loss through hypnotism. Miss A decided to try it. The author discussed her pattern of eating and then, together with a physician, constructed proper balanced meals that would maintain caloric intake at a weight-loss level and still provide the necessary milk therapy for the ulcerous condition. These were called "go" foods. All else were "stop" foods.

She was hypnotized and was told—just as you will tell yourself—that she will no longer crave "stop" foods and will be perfectly satisfied with "go" foods. Her weight started tumbling after the first weekly session. Nine weeks and 53 pounds later, her progress chart started to flatten out.

At this point the hypnotist changed the pattern. His suggestions to her were based on quantity of food. You can be satisfied with less . . . you will feel better if you eat moderately . . . your body does not need as much as you have been giving it . . . etc.

Her weight began to tumble again. She had set a goal of 160 pounds. As she approached this, she set a new goal of 135. She began to dress more fashionably, to fix her hair in the latest style. Her interest in life grew, depressions waned, and even the ulcer attacks became less frequent and intense. She could eat salads and other roughage usually denied to ulcer patients. She had abundant energy for her job. She joined a local swimming club, and a civic organization and was soon socially in demand.

What caused the change in this woman's life? Her subconscious was instructed to motivate her to proper eating habits. She reacted immediately and automatically. It took no self control, no will power. It just happened.

Achieving your second youth

If you were to be more alive, more erect, more attractive to the opposite sex, able to do all that needed to be done during the day with energy and ambition to spare, how else could you describe such a state than as your second youth.

Look at the boundless energy that present-day teenagers have. They are always on the go. They have so much enthusiasm and so few responsibilities that they sometimes channel it into activities that, to say the least, are unproductive. But this energy in your mature hands is like money in the bank.

A 47-year-old editor writes, "Losing ten pounds for me was

like losing 10 years off my age. Just walking was so effortless, I bounced. It was like discovering I had been driving with my brakes on. Naturally, everybody with whom I came into contact noticed the difference in me. I found I could cover twice the ground in my work."

Was it the ten pounds that made all the difference to this man's energy level? It was undoubtedly the major cause. Not just the weight of the body fat lost, though, caused the stepped up vigor. That fat not only weighed, it impeded the normal functioning of other organs. Much of the energy that he is now manifesting was previously being used by the body just to function.

Another factor that helped this man was the magic power of suggestion that actually fired a spirit of go-to-it-iveness in him. He supplemented suggestions to eat properly and act positively. Besides losing ten pounds, he lost the drag of negative attitudes that can short-circuit energy and pump it into a wasteland of worry, anxiety, envy and remorse.

Even without the knowledge of how to talk to *yourself,* which you will learn as you progress in this book, you can still make a start and put your subconscious to work for you through suggestion. One way is to practice looking how you will begin to look when the weight loss gets under way. Stand in front of a full length mirror. Hold you stomach in, shoulders back. Pull yourself up to your full, erect height. Look at yourself front view and both side views. Take a good look, for you will want to remember the image later.

Now go closer to the mirror. Look at your face. Press your double chin back with your hands. Smooth away frown lines. Manipulate jowls and superfluous flesh so that they are not in view and your features are outlined clearly and youthfully. This is another image that you will want to hold in your memory for frequent call-back.

When you are on your way to your right weight using the skilled auto-suggestion methods that you will acquire by means of this book, you will be able to alter dimensions of your body that are now out of proportion due to excessive fat. You can now set the stage for these changes to occur by picturing yourself "in good shape."

The truth is you *will* be "in good shape." You will be able to wear clothes that you could not wear before. Because fashion designers create for the most attractive bodies, most of the overweight people of the country are not able to dress in the latest or most accepted styles. These styles are for the slim. You will be slim. You will be well-dressed. Furthermore, you won't have to discard your handsome new clothes because you have gained back weight lost by temporary measures. You will dress fashionably and look smart—permanently.

The dawn of that great day

Right now, by seeing and believing the image of the new you, by visualizing yourself slim and youthful in appearance, you can bring about the dawn of that new life. As we saw earlier, suggestion works on you whether you want it to or you don't. The television commercial works on you whether you think it is cute or irritating, whether you are in the mood for ice cream or not. If you hear it and see it, the suggestion has been made and is being stored in the subconscious to become part of your future behavior motivation.

If you see it and don't hear it, or if you hear and don't see it, that process will still take place. The suggestion will still reach your subconscious. All it takes is one sensory path, or your own conscious thought. The one essential is that the television or radio set is turned on. You won't be affected by the air waves or by other people talking themselves thin. Your set has to be tuned in to the suggestions of the commercial. Your own voice or imagination must be supplying the suggestions in order for you to be self-affected.

But this will be only the dawn of that great day. It will not shine forth in all its blue sky glory until your learn the short-cut to your subconscious. Without this short-cut you are faced with the time-consuming task of storing up such a vast accumulation of proper eating suggestions and second youth images that their sheer quantity tips the scales. You would actually have to provide as much motivating stimuli as your total environment has provided in past years to make you eat the way you do. Of course, this is almost impossible.

There is a way to beat the power of quantity of environmental suggestions even without knowing the shortcut to the subconscious. It is doubtful you will want to apply this method even if you could figure how to. It has been recently used successfully to treat transvestites—persons afflicted with a compulsion to dress in the clothes of the opposite sex. These persons often wear wigs and make-up to complete the transformation. They often suffer from guilt feelings after doing this. Many have contemplated suicide.

Behavior Research and Therapy, a magazine published in London, recently reported how one man, a 33-year-old government worker, was cured by the aversion technique. At the hospital where he was under treatment, he was taken into a small room and asked to stand on a metal grille. He was then asked to remove his dressing gown and put on his favorite female clothes. At that moment he was given a sharp electric shock through his feet. This provided a memory association so unpleasant that it deterred the bad habit. However, even here quantity had to be supplied—75 times a day for six weeks! Only then did unpleasant memories outweigh the pleasant ones and the habit ended.

Perhaps there is a way to apply this to other areas like homosexuality or in making alcoholics averse to drink. And undoubtedly there is a way to produce a sting, burn, shock or other pain to eventually build up an aversion to carbohydrate indulgences. But one wonders whether the victory of aversion over desire is completely free of repercussions. More likely, it is a collision that can cause the unwanted desire to seek outlets in other directions, perhaps more dangerous than wearing the wrong clothes. The harshness of the shock treatment, admittedly a useful device as a last resort, seems to invite a harsh reaction.

There is no valid reason to use extremes in either quantity or impact for matters involving the drift of daily habits. Giving your subconscious proper direction is a first resort, not a last. It requires neither massive quantity nor harsh contrivance. It's as mild as a conversation and as easy to engage in. It *is* a conversation.

The answer to the impracticality of applying suggestion in quantity and the unacceptability of aversion and shock techniques is self-hypnotism.

Placing yourself in a fully relaxed, almost trance-like state sweeps away the clouds that stand between auto-suggestion and your obedient subconscious, permitting it to see the light instantly. It hears you loud and clear—louder and clearer than scores of commercials, tons of advertising material, and hours of other conscious impressions. It is more than a short-cut to self-mastery. It is the only direct route.

REVIEW

The mirror method for visualizing yourself thin is now a more detailed procedure. Make the various steps outlined on page 66 a regular daily routine. Stop whatever you are doing several times a day and visualize yourself thin, well-dressed, and "in good shape."

5

MAKNG SELF-HYPNOSIS AN EVERYDAY TOOL

The magic key to auto-suggestion is visualization while the mind is in a relaxed state. To visualize is to allow the subconscious to accept the image for storage. To relax is to expose the subconscious more sensitively to this message.

A young woman wanted assistance through hypnotism to rid herself of tension headaches. She brought two girl friends with her to observe. As the hypnologist instructed her to relax and to let her hands and head go limp, she just could not seem to break the tension that gripped her. Patiently the suggestions were given her to relax. Still she seemed to be making only the faintest of efforts. Suddenly there was the sound of snoring. One of the two observers was sitting, hands hanging loosely by her sides, head on her chest, fast asleep. And the other was in the same position!

Anybody can visualize, but not everybody knows the art of relaxation. Your next step in talking yourself thin is to practice the art of relaxation. This practice will pay off for you right now, because in the state of relaxation that you are about to attain, you will give *yourself* a very useful suggestion. You will tell *yourself* that the next time, the relaxation will be faster and deeper. This kind of built in success is one of the reasons why auto-suggestion cannot fail, and why it can easily renew itself and so remain permanent.

Beginning self-hypnotic relaxation

Conduct this exercise in a chair. It will consist of several stages. Read about them first; then try them. In trying them, do Stage 1 first. Then read on, stop, and try Stage 2, and so on.

Practice Stage 1: As soon as you have finished this paragraph, follow the instructions and imagine what is asked of you to imagine. Sit in a straight-back chair. Place your hands on your knees. Close your eyes. Take a deep breath. Exhale, letting your hands drop between your knees and your head sag. There is a pleasant tingle in your hands. Your toes, legs, fingers, arms go limp. Imagine a gray blankness over you. It cuts off the view and permits you to enjoy your relaxed mood in peace. *It is so enjoyable that it will be easy to return to this state again.* Now arouse yourself and feel wide awake and refreshed.

Now read the above paragraph again, visualizing just what you must do; then put the book down and try it.

Practice Stage 2: You may try stage 2 immediately if you wish. You will find it even more delightful than stage 1. In fact it is just a more lengthy version of stage 1 and it will take you a step closer to the kind of true relaxation that will bring you the auto-suggestion results you want.

Again you sit in the chair and permit your arms to sag, your head to droop, and all your body to go limp. Now raise your head and look at a point on the ceiling. Stare at that fixed point on the ceiling. You feel very comfortable. You breathe in slowly, exhale slowly. You become aware of a very comfortable feeling with each breath you take. There's that greyness over you that you saw before. It's like a grey blanket clouding the ceiling. Your whole body begins to feel heavier. First your feet and then your arms. Empty your mind of all thoughts. Know that with each slow breath you are going deeper and deeper into that healthful bliss of total relaxation. *How easy it will be to return to this pleasant state again soon.*

Now you arouse yourself feeling recharged, fine and wide awake.

There is a little more to this stage, as you can see. Perhaps you will like to read it over again. Now put the book down and try it.

Practice Stage 3: To make Stage 3 as easy and pleasant for you as possible, a full conversation with yourself has been prepared. It would be ideal to dictate it into a recorder and play it back to yourself. Or, the right person might help you by reading it to you for the first time or two. But this is not really necessary. You can read it over, committing to memory the general ideas rather than the word-for-word monologue. Are you ready to try it? Then read the following passages:

I am very comfortable ... I am sitting loosely, limply in the chair ... my feet are flat on the floor ... my hands are on my lap or hanging down ... I am very comfortable.

I am looking at the ceiling now ... at a fixed point ... I am staring at the ceiling ... all my attention is focused at the fixed point on the ceiling. My eyelids are getting tired from looking at the point on the ceiling. I am very comfortable. I am taking a slow deep breath and exhaling very slowly ... I am becoming aware of a very comfortable feeling with each breath I take. I am taking another deep breath—I hold it while I count to five and then let it out slowly. One ... two ... three ... four ... five. I enjoy that nice, pleasant, comfortable sensation in my abdomen. As I relax there comes a feeling of heaviness. I feel this heaviness and now I am relaxed.

My eyes are still occupied with the point I have selected on the ceiling. I am becoming aware of my feet ... the soles of my feet are more relaxed ... they are becoming heavier and heavier. My feet are becoming heavier ... moment by moment ... heavier and heavier. The heaviness creeps up into my ankles ... the feet and ankles ... heavier and heavier ...

up the legs into the thighs. My whole body feels heavier and heavier. It is so pleasant and comfortable. The heaviness creeps into the chest . . . up the hands and arms into the neck. Now my whole body from the neck down feels heavy . . . the feet . . . the ankles . . . the legs . . . the thighs . . . the abdomen . . . the chest—heavy—heavy—heavier. My jaws begin to relax . . . the lower jaw relaxes and now my mouth opens slightly . . . My jaws are limp and loose . . . teeth apart . . . lips apart. I am so relaxed my eyelids begin to blink. I will let them blink . . . I will not fight to keep my eyes open . . . I will let them close. I will keep them closed. I will not fight to keep them open . . . I will relax completely . . . I will close them now . . . I will close them and keep them closed.

With my eyes closed . . . I can visualize a darkness—the color grey or black. My mind is empty of thoughts. I am thinking of nothing . . . I am doing nothing. That's the secret of relaxation. I will relax all over now—in my mind and in my body . . . just relax and enjoy the nice comfortable feeling. I will breathe slowly and deeply, exactly as if I were asleep—and with each breath . . . I go deeper . . . deeper and deeper into relaxation . . . deeper and deeper relaxed . . . soon I will be as close to sleep as it's possible to get and yet remain conscious and cooperative. So comfortable . . . breathing slowly and deeply and enjoying every moment.

I know that continuing in this manner will result in hypnosis. It's a pleasant sensation and I know that even in the deepest stage of hypnosis I am no more unconscious than I am now. There will always be an awareness. It's a kind of detached feeling . . . I can ignore what I wish to ignore and pay attention only to what I need and want to pay attention to.

I keep right on relaxing—going deeper and deeper into the trance . . . I am learning to understand with my unconscious mind and I am learning to understand with my conscious mind. I am learning from this experience and will carry it

*into my practice sessions. I can learn by myself through my
own efforts. Now I want time to seem infinitely long, infinitely l-o-n-g and then slowly and gradually I will arouse myself slowly and gradually awake . . . arousing . . . arousing . . .
knowing I can go back again some other time. Arousing . . .
arousing . . . and now all of me has awakened and I feel fine
. . . now I am wide awake. I will move or twist around in the
chair and reorient myself.*

Now put the book down and go through as much of the
monologue and its visualizing as you can remember.

If you're human, you loved it. And one thing is sure,—you
needed it. Some people never take time off to close their eyes
during the day and clear their mind. No wonder the body
adores this intermission from the constant barrage of sensory
communications. Don't get impatient. There will be plenty
of opportunity for more of this fulfilling relaxation. But first
let us exercise our intellect somewhat by trying to understand
just what happens to the conscious and subconscious mind
when you relax.

When you are able to develop your skill at relaxation to
the point where you can enjoy a deep, blissful state, you will
be able to give your control mechanisms positive habit-break-
ing, health-producing suggestions that will take effect immediately. And you will have an advantage over the hypnologist.
You don't have to speak a single word. The conversation can
be a silent one. Your use of image and thought is even better
than the spoken word. It penetrates quickly and deeply into
chambers where are recorded the thousands of words spoken
to you and motivations suggested to you, by package labels,
billboard signs, TV commercials and well-meaning friends.
As a thought image, instead of a spoken word, it will de-mag-
netize the old mentally recorded tapes and re-magnetize them
with your new healthful ideas. The same is true of the relaxation exercises you learned earlier in this chapter. Thinking

that your body is heavy, visualizing the blanket of grey above you is more effective than speaking the words that it is so. In the process of talking yourself thin, the ancient maxim that a picture is worth a thousand words bears repeating again and again.

Understanding the differences between hypnosis and auto-hypnosis

A hypnologist can put you on the right tack food-wise. Or you can do it yourself. If you do it, you will be using auto-hypnosis. It is capable of all the same astounding effects as hypnosis. It is one and the same. In both cases you are reaching the deep unconscious and flashing images which produce automatic effects.

For those persons who would not let themselves be hypnotized, for one reason or another, auto-hypnosis is usually perfectly acceptable. Some consider it imprudent to expose their secret control centers to the will of another. Others, who know little about hypnosis, fear that its use may be dangerous to their mental facilities. For these people, hypnosis and auto-hypnosis are not one and the same. In auto-hypnosis there is no other will involved than your own. There is no state of mind involved other than what you experience in some degree many times during the day; for instance, when you are relaxed in an armchair and concentrating on a spot on the wall known as television, or like when you are relaxed on your bed just before dropping off to sleep.

Those who have these fears or reservations about hypnotism need have no such concern about self-hypnotism or auto-suggestion. You are the captain of your own ship, the master of your soul. The cataleptic-like trances into which hypnotized subjects can be put are not part of the procedure of talking yourself thin.

Instead, auto-hypnosis is just a restful quieting of the mind, a way of putting your busy thoughts aside so that certain thoughts, important to you, can enter the subconscious where they can work permanently for your better health. This restful quieting of the mind is similar to the art of quiet meditation used in religious and spiritual devotion. Meditation cleanses the mind, opens its pores to pure elevated ideas. Meditation builds vigor by removing the negative fears and thoughts that act as roadblocks to energy and inspiration.

When you relax, as you did earlier in this chapter, you do all of these wonderful things for yourself. And it takes no more than a few minutes. In this state of relaxation your mind is receptive to, even greedy for, all the positive, constructive images you can send its way. There is nothing mystical or mysterious about this. This is normal, successful living. This is one of the reasons why wealthy people, who in their relaxed moments think of their wealth, get wealthier. And it is why people who contemplate their poverty, get poorer. It is why active people, who in their quiet moments visualize their next activities, acquire boundless energy to act. And why sluggish people who contemplate obstacles and limitations, bog down. It also helps the fat person to get fatter, but will help you, by properly directing your relaxed moments, to get thinner.

Why, then, go into all of these physical phenomena induced by hypnotism? Because, it helps us to understand the great scope of suggestive power, the better to use it. If you do not have this knowledge, you might labor under disbelief. To be incredulous, is to bring about what you believe and imagine —failure. On the other hand, to understand the powers being used, is to know it must work for you and to insure success. Furthermore, understanding suggestion and hypnosis helps us to fit it into the framework of our everyday behavior and to use it wisely in the furtherance of self-mastery.

How your subconscious motivates you to eat what you eat

If you were at a party and the hostess approached and asked if you would care for some bombones de arroz, What would you say? Probably you would ask cautiously, "What is it?" On the other hand, if she approached you with this delicacy on a tray, you would know it was food. Because it was a party, you would be sure it was a festive or gourmet food. Your hand would reach out adventurously, your imagination would expect a repeat of past pleasant taste sensations, and your saliva would begin to flow. Our environment and surroundings are constantly being interpreted by our subconscious in the framework of its vast file of past experiences.

If you had previously tasted bombones de arroz, you would know immediately that it was a Spanish delicacy and you would know whether you liked it or not. If you found it not to your taste, the mere mention of the name would prevent the salivary flow. The sight of it would flash the signal "no." No reaching, no expectation of gustatory pleasure, no salivary reaction, "No, thanks."

If you had previously found bombones de arroz to be delicious, you would not have to work at generating an appetite, or at alerting your taste buds, or at getting your mouth set for it. This would all happen automatically even if you were on a diet. In fact, just the imagining of this pleasure now is probably causing your mouth to water. As hard as you tried, you could not get your mouth to water by command; but visualize a sizzling steak on a platter, covered with broiled mushrooms and—the deluge.

Will your mouth water, too, at the sight of home-made deep-dish apple pie topped with a mound of melting vanilla ice cream? Sure it will. If you are overweight, your critical conscious viewpoint interjects "no." The battle of willpower is then joined. Which will prevail? The conscious "no," or the willing hand; expectant taste buds, and watering mouth.

You know better than anyone else. If conscious will power has won on many an occasion, subconscious urge has won on many, many more. In the long run, it is the subconscious that moves your knife and fork, despite all your reasoning and calorie-counting to the contrary. The trick is to get to your subconscious and re-train it.

How to check your progress

How can you tell that you are getting through to your subconscious? How do you know for sure *you* are listening? The answer to this question is always "You *are* getting through." The only question is one of degree. Even that quick, "I must get up at 6:45 A.M.," has its astounding on-the-minute results. You can increase the degree of these results by deepening your relaxation before giving the instructions. This gradually eases the conscious to the background, leaving the subconscious free of interference. Hypnosis is often defined as that state in which suggestion is more effective than usual.

After you have practiced the relaxation exercises given in the early part of this chapter for several times, you will be ready for a simple suggestion that, on the count of ten, you will reach the deep state of relaxation that previously took a certain amount of mental discipline. You will see how well you are reaching *yourself* when this countdown suggestion exerts its post-hypnotic effect and you drift immediately into that blissful state.

Then your mind will be free to devote itself to the business of the moment: giving yourself suggestions on how you feel toward "stop" foods and how you feel toward "go" foods. You will know immediately—during your next meal—that you are getting through to *yourself*. You will take instant pride in your achievement. You will recognize then, better than you can possibly imagine now, how you have suddenly come face to face with *yourself*—and that *you* are a pretty easy person to get along with, after all.

You will also understand that the mysterious subconscious is really not so mysterious after all, and that auto-hypnosis is no strange, trance-like ritual, but merely the workings of everyday laws of thought and behavior. You will have no fear of deep relaxation. You will know how to remain alert to any emergency and how to avoid falling asleep during relaxation. You will know to make your suggestion "stick" so that it does its good work for months, and you will know how to build into your suggestions automatic instructions for their periodic reinforcement.

So will the countdown method of inducing instant relaxation bring you to the threshold of self-mastery and a permanently controlled waist-line. And it is only pages away.

Before you start the next chapter, practice the relaxation procedures on pages 72-75 once more. Read it through, put the book down, and let go.

REVIEW

Practice Stage 1 and Stage 2 once more. Then go on to Stage 3. There is no need to use Stage 1 or Stage 2 again. They are merely stepping stones to Stage 3, which is your principle relaxation monologue to use in talking yourself thin.

6

HOW TO "DIAGNOSE"
YOUR OWN CASE
AND FIGHT YOUR FAT

Scores of books in the self-help field in recent years have pointed up the incredible power of the human mind: the power to make prayers come true, the power to sell successfully, the power to heal, to create valuable ideas, to increase memory 100%, to win friends and become influential.

Millions who have read them have come at least one step closer to the wealth, contentment, happiness and health that are the promise of these books. Thousands of others have benefited immensely, bringing about dramatic changes in their life. Some lesser number have witnessed that miraculous transformation that vaults them to lofty heights of self-mastery —and, incidentally, potential authorship of another self-help book.

Why does not every reader attain the miracle? Is it the fault of the reader or the book? What will be the percentage of success of this book?

This book has a new ingredient: through the relaxation technique that you began to practice in the last chapter, it can spoon-feed your mind! It can channel its skills deep into the recesses of your subconscious where this knowledge takes its place alongside of mannerisms, habits, attitudes, beliefs,

1

and knowledge which you have collected through the years. Practicing its skills becomes part of your way of life, long after the book has been forgotten. New, healthful, appetite-satisifying eating ways are donned like your favorite suit or dress.

Thus, this book has a high success factor built right into it. All you have to do is to punctuate your reading with occasional relaxation sessions, using each session to help quicken and deepen your next session, and using each session also to improve your desire to talk yourself thin. This chapter will take you another step toward full self-hypnotic relaxation.

One of the unexplained phenomena of the mind is used universally in psycho-therapy: with understanding comes cure. Explain the cause behind a symptom and the symptom often disappears.

Understanding why he overeats will go a long way toward making the average person wiser about food. It can be parlayed into a tremendous pay-off in poundage lost, when combined with suggestions for proper eating.

Write your own case history

Scores of case histories can be related illustrating the emotional causes behind overeating, but you would not necessarily recognize yourself in any of them. No two lives are identical. Major similarities may exist, but minor differences in environment can change behavior patterns considerably.

Only your case history can disclose the reasons behind your eating the way you do. So why not write it yourself? Psychologists have found this type of writing a valuable doorway to inner motivations. All you do is sit down with pad and pencil and write the story of your weight. Start back in your teens if you can. Trace how your weight changed, how you felt about it, what you did about it? Describe each period of your life; was it a happy time, changing time, difficult time.

Read this case history through. It was written by a woman while undergoing hypno-therapy:

I am 38 years old; when I was 18 our family doctor, hoping to stop my steadily increasing weight gain, gave me some pills to help curb my appetite. Facing up to it now for the very first time I realized that I have rarely, if ever, been without some sort of pill since that first time. Years of different doctors, and different pills, but always the same results. The first flush of enthusiasm as the medicine seemed to be working, the gradual cheating which inevitably followed the first weight loss, and then the depression over the steadily returning pounds—a depression which called for more eating to counteract it. Thus I would come full circle within months, sometimes weeks, of starting the diet.

My trouble has always been spasmodic, rather than steady overeating. I would eat almost normally for a few days, and then go on a binge of such monumental proportions that very often I'd pray that I would get sick enough to remember the next time.

I was married at 22, took reducing pills before the wedding, gained back the weight on my honeymoon. I gained 32 pounds with my first child, and while this was still partially with me, I gained 25 with my second. Marital and family pressures sent me running to the refrigerator, but the increase in weight only made me harder to live with and my problems more intense.

Finally at 198½ pounds, our family physician gave me the name of a doctor who specialized in "obesity."

This was my first contact with a doctor specializing in overweight, but not my last. Right from the beginning the method seemed made in heaven for me. Pills all day long; all the foods I liked to eat and in quantity, pills to curb my appetite, pills to anti-depress me, pills to counteract the anti-depressant and vitamins. I lost 50 pounds in less than 4 months. But as soon as I stopped the pills, the old cravings returned. And, slowly, so did the weight.

So it went. Over the past six years I have spent anywhere from two to five months of the year practicing my "preventive medicine"—averaging about $200.00 a year. Seeing it written down is kind of shocking, but up to now it seemed the only way.

Then began a chain of events which I feel now was the best thing that ever happened to me. A back injury about three years old finally necessitated surgery. Naturally, I went back on the pills because I didn't want to go into hospital too heavy. I went in at 160 pounds, and emerged after almost an entire winter of immobility at 181 pounds.

Again the pills, only this time the magic formula was gone. Nothing was wrong with the system—just with me. I was so satiated with drugs that the strongest had no effect; besides it was much easier to eat and feel sorry for myself. Even the shell I was used to crawling into was getting a little snug. I really felt I had no place to turn. What was left except revising my whole way of life and thought, and learning to control my cravings. I thought I was not capable of doing without drugs—the drugs that no longer worked for me.

A remark by a casual friend led me to hypnosis, and I'm afraid I went into it carrying, besides my weight, a big fat chip on my shoulder. I'd had all the usual warnings from people who knew even less than I did, but within a short time I found my doubts allayed and my original skepticism completely gone. A small glimmer of hope began to appear and I felt as though I were being given a chance to be reborn. Sounds dramatic? I guess so, but how else do you put it when you get a chance to salvage a life that was of no earthly use to anyone, least of all to yourself.

After a few sessions I no longer ask, "Can it last?" I know it will last, just as I know that I'm becoming a breathing, functioning woman again. In a short space of time I have felt the tight knot of anger that has been inside of me ever since this weight battle began, begin to dissolve and disappear. This is not to say that I don't still get angry or depressed, but I don't use each incident as an excuse for a tirade or an eating binge. Because I no longer need the food as compensation, I turn to something stimulating to take my mind off whatever is bothering me. I eat normal meals, and when I am through eating a moderate amount I am no longer hungry. It is as simple as that. No more senseless craving and going from food to food to fill an unfillable chasm—the lacks in my life, real and imaginary, no longer send me running for the leftovers.

The weight loss is being accomplished most painlessly. For the very first time in my entire life I am eating three meals a day and losing weight without pills. It is no longer too much trouble for me to fix the proper food for myself and my family because along with the weight loss has come increased stimulation and energy. Now my mind is so much brighter, and my disposition and physical being follow suit. Food has become important only to appease actual hunger (something which is accomplished quite easily), and I find my taste buds actually coming alive again after years of just swallowing.

I am beginning to place the value on myself that a woman should have; suddenly I am beginning to have self-respect and self-assuredness again.

It's as though all my perceptions were heightened, and in this new found clarity, I like what I see.

Isn't this a splendid self-analysis? How often do we get a chance to stop and take a long, long look at ourselves in a crystal clear mirror. Writing it down this way, like a letter to yourself, helps. It can be very useful to all of us as we begin to talk ourselves thin. Resolve now to give it a try soon. It was useful to this woman. It helped to illuminate the nature of her emotional stresses and to give her an insight into the corrective attitudes. Understanding initiates a change for the better.

Talk sense to yourself

The better you know yourself, the wiser and more understanding you will be when you put yourself under your own control and make use of the enormous proven power of hypnotic suggestion. You are now at the stage where you are mastering the art of relaxation. The suggestions that you are giving yourself while relaxed are directed at quickening and deepening the powers of relaxation.

The step after that will be to give yourself suggestions for a new, healthful way of eating. The amazing changes that will occur immediately in complete obedience to your word will start you thinking. You will be tempted to free yourself of life-wrecking fears and guilts, to conquer unhappy moods and depressions, to rid yourself of mental blocks, to end chronic aches and pains, and perhaps to improve your skills, memory or business acumen. Once you see auto-hypnotism work on your life in the eating department, you cannot help but want to apply its "magic" power to assist you in other ways.

Research in auto-conditioning conducted at Duke University over a number of years, led by Dr. Hornell Hart, proved that people can control their moods through self-hypnosis. Those prone to prolonged periods of gloom and acute depths of depression were able to shift their whole level of happiness several steps higher by the relaxation and suggestion technique. Dramatic improvements were recorded in courage, efficiency, enthusiasm, success, health, and friendliness.

The key to realizing dramatic changes for the better in your life lies to a large degree in your ability to distinguish between positive and negative emotions. If, in writing your case history, you found you were describing your over-riding attitude as one of envy or fear, certainly you recognize these as negative feelings. If your life became dominated for a period by feelings of love and enthusiasm, surely you recognize these as positive emotions.

A rule to follow in measuring the polarity of an emotion is whether it is creative or destructive. Friendliness is creative, animosity is destructive. Fear is destructive, confidence is creative.

When you are relaxed and are ready to give yourself suggestions to improve your total well-being, you must always suggest an end to negative emotions and the strengthening of positive emotions.

Here are some more examples of negative feelings, attitudes and emotions: remorse, envy, jealousy, hate, anger, anxiety, self-contempt, worry, failure, apprehension, distrust, helplessness, pessimism, boredom, apathy, impotence, weariness, frustration, malevolence, disbelief. That may be the most negative sentence ever written but there are many more negative facets to our collective personalities. Perhaps you can think of a few more.

Here are some more examples of positive feelings, attitudes and emotions: faith, love, trust, security, understanding, strength, boldness, success, optimism, self-approval, interest, awareness, zest, vitality, alertness, cheerfulness, gratitude, benevolence, appreciation, thoughtfulness.

Everything in the previous negative list seems synonymous with sickness and failure and reeks of evil. Note that we have ended on a positive note. If we had ended on a negative note, it would have been leaving you with a negative residual suggestion, destructive in nature. By ending on the positive note, you are left with a constructive, creative thought. This is the technique to use in talking sense to *yourself*.

If you are an over-weight salesman, you may find it helpful to augment the proper eating suggestions, which you will learn later in this book, with suggestions that end thoughts of failure and instead encourage thoughts of opportunity and challenge.

If you are an overweight housewife, you may respond to proper eating suggestions more readily and lose weight faster if you discover your negative thoughts—those of boredom, futility, or depression—and supplant them with suggestions of zest, purpose, and reward.

The same approach applies to the business man who seeks affluence in food and finds his tycoonship in a big abdominal corporation; or the unpopular girl who substitutes a full stomach for a full sex-life; or the lonely housewife who strikes up a platonic friendship with her refrigerator. Understanding yourself does not cause you to lose weight, but it is nonetheless an integral part of the overweight cure.

Attack the carbohydrates

No matter how well you know yourself, and no matter how good you are at discerning your negative attitudes and replacing them through auto-suggestion with positive attitudes, you will probably still be faced with a scale that reads "overweight." You will have done yourself an immense good in the personality department and prepared yourself for a rapid response to the new way of eating when it comes, but you will not start the scale drifting down until you break your present eating habits. That break will come with no more effort than you have already shown by reading these words and practicing the relaxation exercises. The eating suggestions you give yourself will do the weighty work. The personality suggestions you give yourself will do other necessary work to make you a happier and more effective person as your weight drifts down. It is work that needs doing and work that you will not be able to resist doing when you see just how easy it is. However, it would be a mistake to think that personality suggestions will replace the results of the carbohydrate suggestion bombardment. Positive suggestions can replace negative suggestions and it will be like taking your foot off the brake and stepping on the gas. But it takes protein suggestions to replace carbohydrate suggestions, and knock weight off.

A 42-year-old unmarried woman who worked in an insurance office found that she was steadily gaining weight. She could stay on a diet just so long and then—whoosh! She would catch up in the carbohydrates she missed. This woman was afraid of losing her job. Every time there was a dispute or uncomfortable time with her supervisor she would comfort herself with food. Suggestions were given her of security and self-reliance, and they overcame her fears. Suggestions of understanding and harmony removed her tendency toward misunderstanding and discord. But she did not lose weight. She had gradually acquired undesirable eating habits. She was a happier, more relaxed person, but she still enjoyed the danish pastry at coffee break. She became fast friends with the other woman, her superior, who had appeared the villain in the case, and they enjoyed having lunch together—but it was the same carbohydrate lunch that she used to eat alone. The case was not closed until she was also given suggestions that changed her eating habits back to the way she used to eat before she got the job.

What would have happened to this woman if she was given the corrective eating suggestions without the correct personality suggestions? Would she have lost weight? Would she have sought comfort from her insecurity in other directions —perhaps in men? Yes, she would have lost weight, but everything else would have remained the same. She would still be miserable and still seek comfort in food: different food; salads instead of potatoes, fruits instead of fruit pies. If food had been removed from her life through suggestion, she would have had to substitute something in its place. Of course it is impossible to quit eating permanently. On the other hand, had excessive smoking been her comfort, she could have stopped that and chances are strong that she would have had to substitute something in its place.

The moral: give yourself calorie suggestions first. Then back them up and with positive, pump-priming personality suggestions.

Count-down to the subconscious

We are now ready to take the next step in bringing on a deep state of relaxation. It requires that you have already seated yourself comfortably in a chair and practiced the dialogue technique in the previous chapter. This is called the count-down method and it will get you to that blissful state in a matter of seconds.

Once there, you will take advantage of a few minutes with *yourself* in three ways. You will suggest that the next time your relaxation will be deeper and faster. You will suggest that the next time *you* will be even more receptive to your suggestions. And finally you will suggest that when you end the session you will be wide-awake, re-vitalized and . . . (here is where you inject a positive attitude.) Pick one which you think could use re-enforcing in your own personality, i.e.— more secure, self-reliant, courageous, confident, trusting, understanding, loving, forgiving.

Here is how the count-down method works. You sit in your comfortable chair. It is located in a quiet room. The lights are dim. Nothing can disturb or distract you. A sense of joyous serenity descends over you. You are ready to let yourself go.

You stare at the ceiling, focusing your attention at a fixed point. You are very comfortable. You remember how this was the beginning of a deeply relaxed state. Picture yourself in this beginning stage again and give it a number. Number ten.

Your eyelids are getting tired. You take a slow deep breath, exhaling very slowly. This, too, you did before on your way to deep relaxation. Visualize this state as number nine.

With each deep breath you take, you sink deeper and deeper. There is that nice pleasant comfortable sensation in your abdomen. Number eight.

There comes that feeling of heaviness. Your feet are becoming heavier. Up the legs into the thighs. Your whole body feels heavier. Number seven.

The jaws begin to relax. Your mouth opens slightly. Your eyes blink. Visualize this stage as number six.

Your eyes close. This is the half-way mark. Number five.

You visualize darkness. Mind is emptied of thought. Number four.

Enjoyment of the relaxed feeling occupies your being. Number three.

Deeper and deeper. Even deeper than before. Number two.

Now time seems infinitely long. Number one.

In this state you tell *yourself* that the numbers ten to one will carry you back the same path to even deeper depths the next time.

In this state you tell *yourself* that *you* will have a heightened suggestibility the next time, that every thought will be accepted readily and confidently.

In this state, you tell *yourself* of the need to be more positive in the way which you have decided will be good for you.

In this state, you tell *yourself* that when you count one through ten you will arouse, totally, completely, feeling wide awake and re-charged.

That is it. What you do by this count-down method is associate a number with each stage of relaxation, so that by just repeating the numbers you reach that stage. You were promised a simple built-in method of using auto-suggestion to improve itself. This is it. You do not have to follow it word for word. In fact, you can divide the process of relaxation in ten other ways than it is done here. The results will be the same. You will picture each stage as you reach it. Give it a number. Following the suggestions for improvement and a suggestion regarding the reverse count, you give the count and out you come.

The next time all you do is assume the position and in ten

second counts you are enjoying an even deeper relaxation than before. Soon you will even be able to count by two's!

Now read the count-down method over again. Visualize the ten stages so that you etch them in your memory. Then put the book down and try it.

REVIEW

Write your case history. Then be your own analyst. What emotional causes might have been behind your over-eating? Look at them objectively and counsel yourself on what your proper attitude might have been. Write this counsel down, briefly. The words can later be used as suggestive means for self-improvement. Be sure to practice the countdown method until all you need to do to attain instant relaxation is count to ten.

7

HOW TO DEVELOP A STRONGER, MORE LASTING POWER OF SUGGESTION

You have been asked to listen to that still small voice that falsely calls itself hunger and to identify its true colors. Once you know it for what it is—insecurity, boredom, or any of these basic sub-conscious emotions—the masquerade ball is over. But the dangerous music can, and will, linger on.

The music of starches and sweets must be stilled in the sub-conscious. A different, more life-giving music, must be instilled in its place.

The time has come. The true power of suggestion must now be unveiled to you. This chapter will set the stage for your skillful use of this power, by giving you a clear understanding of it. If you understand just how far you can go in ordering a particular behavior, you will be able to govern your suggestions accordingly. You will also understand where you cannot go.

How to hate pastry

Now conduct the relaxation exercise you learned at the beginning of Chapter 5. You may make whatever changes in the procedure which you find feasible. You should use the elevator method of deepening the relaxation if you have already practiced it. If not, you may relax comfortably and deeply in a chair, using the monologue on pages 73-75 as a basis. Before you begin, read on until you are given instructions to begin.

When you reach the blissful state of deep, peaceful relaxation, you will visualize one of your mortal enemies—pastry. Instead of being conquered by it, you will see yourself conquering it, refusing it, passing it up for life-giving, mineral-rich melon and grapefruit.

Here is a suggestion to use that will conquer pastry, thus removing one of the biggest cannons in the carbohydrate bombardment to which you are being subjected. Read it, believe it, absorb it, use it:

Pastry represents fat and ugliness. To eat pie, pastry, or cake is to eat fat and ugliness. I can imagine the pastry turning into fat in my mouth, trickling down my throat and depositing itself as a thick and ugly layer of fat in my body.

Instead of putting this fat and ugliness in my mouth, I will have as my dessert a delicious portion of succulent melon or tangy grapefruit. I can imagine myself slim, slender, and satisfied.

Do not memorize the above words. Instead, let your mind entertain the thoughts as you read them. Then go over the thoughts again in your mind: imagine the pastry as fat; picture it trickling down your throat and sticking to your stomach; imagine yourself eating the melon instead and enjoying its succulent, slenderizing taste.

If there is anything about this succession of thoughts that still causes them to falter as you think them, there is a chance that you are not completely ready to accept them. In order for any suggestion to work, it must have assured, non-critical acceptance. There must be no shadow of a doubt that you will be thinner, more attractive, more successful, and healthier with a melon coffee break than with a pastry coffee break. There is little that you can do for yourself if you are not ready to accept the need to be thinner. Suppose you weigh 200 pounds, and you would like to weigh 135 pounds. If you cannot see yourself weighing 135 pounds you may never reach it. You are putting yourself in a class with persons who say "I can't see myself doing that." And they don't do it.

On the other hand, this suggestion may sound so good to you and you may be so anxious for it to get started and to be effective that you would like it to be even stronger. If so, here is a technique to follow. Think it over before you decide to use it, though; it is powerful.

Use any abhorrent image as a tool

What do you abhor? Disorder, sweat, insects? Add a measure or two of abhorrence to your visual image of pie as fat. See it baked with roaches in it or served with sore-ridden hands. There is no need to explain to you why this works. It puts pie and cake into the same appetite category as stewed cat, served hair and all. It draws a cancel sign through all the appetizing slogans that have conditioned you, and re-conditions you with disgust.

Do not use the above at first. Save it for use only to help things along, if later you find you need a booster. Disgust, used in a post-hypnotic suggestion, may manifest as real disgust at the time it motivates. In other words, you may be disgusted at the sight of pie or cake and actually visualize the abhorrent scenes you used to condition yourself. There is no need to do this to yourself. You will act comfortably without it. You will automatically desire grapefruit in preference to the pie, without consciously knowing your auto-conditioning is at work.

If you do find it necessary to introduce the abhorrence factor as a booster, chances are your suggestibility is such that no conscious disgust will be evident to you.

Read over the suggestion on the previous page once more. As soon as you reach the deep stage of relaxation, visualize the pie that "melts in your mouth"—as fat. Now get into your favorite relaxation chair and begin.

Factors influencing suggestions

You have taken the first step to change your eating habits effortlessly through suggestion. Later you will learn how to broaden that step by deepening your relaxation, increasing your skill at auto-suggestion, and substituting right foods for wrong foods all the way down the line.

But first let us examine what you have just done. You have sat down in a chair, concentrated your attention on a fixed spot, relaxed with a heaviness technique, deepened your relaxation through an elevator technique, instructed yourself to avoid the fattening effect of pie and cake and instead to enjoy the thinning effect of melon and grapefruit. You also suggested that the next time you will relax even deeper and quicker. You then aroused yourself, feeling fine and energetic, and now you are reading again.

Will it work after this one session? If so, for how long? The answer is: It *must* work. It *is* working. The degree and length of effectiveness depends on several factors. If we understand these factors, we can use them to improve and extend the successful effect.

Factor # 1: Perhaps the most important of these factors is the noncritical acceptance just referred to. Doctors know that a patient who believes he cannot be cured is the worst patient. The negative belief can actually stave off the healing process. Confidence, coupled with the will to live, can bring about miracles in recovery. A patient must be convinced that he will recover, for treatment to have its optimum benefit.

Suppose impotency was the problem. The suggestion is given: "I will no longer be plagued by sexual impotence. Instead, I will enjoy normal sexual relations." Will it work?

For the man who knows that he has lost the virility that once moved him, it will not work. For the man who knows that he is still the man he once was, but is only being temporarily blocked by some emotional debris, it will work.

The importance of this conviction cannot be overstated. In cases where conviction has been backed by a high-pitched emotional expectation, the results are phenomenal. In hypnotism, the therapist's positive attitude produces a state of expectation in the subject. His radiating confidence fills the subject with the non-critical acceptance necessary to success. In self-hypnotism, you must be prepared by "operation bootstrap"—either by reading the first preparatory chapters again, or by auto-conditioning yourself in numerous relaxation periods to an attitude of confidence and optimism in your slimming success.

Factor # 2: Another factor of importance is the size of the behavior step that you are suggesting be taken. A small step is easier than a giant one. For instance, a young man who stammers visualizes himself speaking to an audience of 5,000 in Carnegie Hall. He suggests to himself that this is the way things can and should be. Is he successful? Hardly. Aside from the incredulity he himself must feel, it is too abrupt a behavior change to ask for. It will more likely encourage conflict and possibly even create more stutter-causing tension. The proper procedure for this man is to start from where he is now and to move forward in small stages. Does he talk to animals without stuttering? Then he should visualize his best friend listening to him talk to his dog. He has brought one person into his stutter-free life. Perhaps he should then visualize his family in the picture, and so forth. In this way, a path is built around the emotional debris that causes this impediment and permits normal behavior to flow around it.

The person who is talking himself thin should follow this same procedure, setting sensible weight loss goals that he or she knows can be reached in a reasonable time.

Factor #3: Another factor affecting suggestibility success is the "as if" attitude. When you visualized the carbohydrate-filled pie dripping down your throat as fat and sticking to your ribs, did you do so as a technique, or did you do so "as if" it were true. Remember the person with rose fever who sneezed at the plastic roses? They looked to that person as if they were real roses. Suggestions will "work" only if they are accepted as if they were true. The fact that the carbohydrate in the seven-layer cake must be ingested and digested before it can become fat, and does not really go the direct route as visualized, must not be given the logical, realistic approach. Your natural desire for the rational must yield to the expediency of the image. The end result is true; so must the symbolism be accepted as if it were true.

Mechanics of suggestion

At least one manufacturer of learn-while-you-sleep records has realized the potential of the awake but relaxed mind. A set of records for daytime use teaches habit control. The lesson is engraved on the relaxed mind, says the manufacturer, no need to take notes, all you do is relax and carefully listen.

If the mental engraving process was that accessible, this would be a strange world. Every message would erase the previous one or supersede it. We would respond to every advertising message, accede to every suitor, switch political belief with every speech. The jury would convict or exonerate depending on whether the district attorney or defense attorney spoke last. Fortunately, we have a layer of conscious grey matter through which all sensory stimuli must pass. Our conscious judgment evaluates, weighs and classifies. It also acts as a cushion or resistor, diminishing the loud exhortations of the outside world so that by the time they are etched in the subconscious they are but a whisper among whispers.

The recording, played to the relaxed mind that listens carefully, can do little more educating than can the ordinary good teacher who addresses an attentive, relaxed student. The lesson must still make its way through the critical consciousness and end up as a mark on a report card.

The mechanics of mental engraving requires that the cushion of consciousness be folded aside so that the acid of suggestion can touch the metal of subconscious mind. Not only must there be a boring of the subconscious, but there must be a pouring of the acid. Packaged in the bottle of a textbook, recording, or teacher's voice it is but the shadow of acid. It will not etch. Pour it into the container of your mind in the liquid flow of mind-image, mind-thought and mind-belief, and the image, thought, and belief become truly etched. Such suggestions remain permanently engraved in the nerve center that runs you.

Your motivation center

Perhaps the most dramatic results of learning through hypnosis are those achieved by hypnosis and self-hypnosis in etching over an unwanted impression and causing even about-face behaviors to be motivated. Known as post-hypnotic suggestions, these behaviors are induced in hypnosis and self-hypnosis with equal ease.

Once accepted, a post-hypnotic suggestion becomes a compulsion. The compulsion will continue to exert its pressure until release by physical action. If you get the thought that you would like to go to the freezer and have some ice cream, you may be able to resist that urge at least temporarily. A post-hypnotic suggestion will badger you even harder and coerce you faster. Suppose a subject is given the post-hypnotic suggestion that at the stroke of noon, tomorrow, he will remove his shoes. Let some one say it is noon, and the shoes will come off no matter what time it is. Obviously, post-hypnotic suggestions as baseless as this example should not be indulged in.

Why you can't include time in your suggestions

In changing our eating-motivations, no such dramatic time element can be introduced safely. It would not do to suggest "you will not be hungry until noon." We *can* suggest that our new list of "go" foods will be entirely satisfying. This usually suffices to tone down quantity and make normal portions as filling as former gluttonous ones. We can also give the type of "disgust" post-hypnotic suggestions described earlier in this chapter, suggestions in your relaxed state which will later make candy taste like burnt rubber. The most valuable result of post-hypnotic suggestion in diet control is the reversing of motivations so that the red light shines on the cakes and pies where once the green light shone, and the green light says go to melon and grapefruit instead.

The subject is seldom aware after hypnosis that he is responding to a post-hypnotic suggestion. Ask the subject why he removed his shoes. He will not connect the act with it being noon. Nor will he say he was hypnotized into doing it. He will have felt as if he acted spontaneously and will attribute his motivations to a spur-of-the-moment whim, or an "I just felt like it" attitude.

This is the beauty of the auto-hypnotic control of eating habits. There is no recall of the relaxation session and the suggestions given. The next time you choose grapefruit instead of pie, it won't be through a conscious struggle. It will be a spur-of-the-moment or "I just felt like it" attitude. It may not be until you are half-way through the grapefruit that you will realize what has happened. You will then become one of the thousands who have enjoyed the thrill of knowing that they are off the treadmill and on the permanent road to trim figures at long last.

Each time you relax more and faster

Another post-hypnotic suggestion which you have given yourself will also manifest itself unobserved and unobtrusively; perhaps it has already done so. This is the suggestion that the next time you relax, you will do so deeper and faster. Give this post-hypnotic suggestion credit for part of your next success. Use it again and again as an automatic step in your auto-conditioning procedure.

The secret doorway to the subconscious

The wonders of the subconscious and its control over the physical senses and organs of the body have been known to medical science for centuries, but that knowledge has never been fully utilized in devising therapy for mental or physical disorders. Even the progress of the past decade has brought us to but the threshold of this vast area. We have the knowledge now to do for ourselves the miracles of self-improvement and self-mastery for which man has always yearned. We need to know little more than the location of the secret door to this powerful subconscious. Once opened, how it works its magic matters little. The only thing that does matter is that we seek to conjure white magic from it and not black magic; that we turn its implicit obedience to the good of our health and our spirit and give the spark that moves it the awesome respect it merits.

The secret door lies just behind the conscious thought that you are now experiencing as you read these lines. Stop that thought, divert it to meaningless dot on the wall, and hold it there incommunicado and you stand at the vestibule of the great subconscious. If you have been diligent about following the relaxation exercises given so far and have also given yourself the suggestions provided, you have opened your secret door to the subconscious and have seen it work its power in your behalf. Practice makes perfect. If your enthusiasm to read along has interfered with that practice, the next chapter will be the real beginning for you as it gives you session after session of easy techniques to try out so that you can be sure you have found the way to fold back your conscious and open that secret door.

REVIEW

Practice your relaxation. When thoroughly relaxed give yourself the "fat and ugliness" suggestions that throw the light of truth on the nature of carbohydrates. Expand them to include not just pastry, but also all dough products and sweets. If you want to put more truth into this suggestion, try one of the "disgusting" techniques mentioned or invent one of your own.

8

SELECTING THE RIGHT
INDUCTION TECHNIQUE

By the time you have tried the different relaxation-inducing techniques in this chapter and practiced the one that really "sends" you, you will be ready to start a vigorous examination of food. This will not be a calorie-hunting expedition, but rather a battle to exterminate the carbohydrate from your eating habit. You will then be able to hold your new way of culinary life in your hand while in deep relaxation, tell yourself, "this is it." And it most certainly will be.

She kept a record

A 37-year-old, 174-pound woman was at the same stage as you—ready to learn deep relaxation and then to suggest proper eating routines after an interview prior to her first hypnosis session, she was asked to keep a record of her food intake for the next week, so that a comparison could be made of the changes that would soon be occurring. Here is the actual record for the first 24 hours:

> *Tuesday 1:00 P.M.:* Left Mr. Petrie's office, stopped luncheonette. Had 12 ounces of lentil soup with 10 oysterettes; 2 poached eggs on 2 slices of buttered white toast; 8 ounces of milk; a cup of coffee with milk and 1½ teaspoons of sugar.

Tuesday 6:15 P.M.: While walking to train; did some window shopping, passed pizza place, had 2 slices, 2 cups of coffee with milk and sugar.

Tuesday 8:30 P.M.: Home for dinner, ½ pound broiled rib steak; 1 slice white bread with butter; ½ cup peas and carrots; 2 plums, 1 peach, 1 nectarine; 2 eight ounce glasses of apple juice.

Tuesday 10:30 P.M.: About 12 ounces of cold beet soup and sour cream.

Wednesday 10:15 A.M.: Bowl of dry cereal with 8 ounces of milk; 2 teaspoons of sugar; 1 nectarine.

Wednesday 11:00 A.M.: 3 cups of coffee with milk and sugar.

Wednesday 1:30 P.M.: Large portion of beef stew with natural gravy, peas and carrots, potatoes; large salad, tomato, cucumber, olive oil; 8 ounces of apple juice.

Wednesday 3:30 P.M.: Large salad, olive oil; 1 slice of white bread, 1 cup thick strained vegetable soup; small portion of meat.

Wednesday 4:30 P.M.: 8 ounces of apple juice.

Wednesday 5:00 P.M.: Large portion of watermelon.

One week later, this woman had been taught deep relaxation to the point where she could quickly and easily reach a pleasant trance-like state. She had agreed on a list of "go" foods, low in carbohydrates, and a list of prohibited "stop" foods heavy in fat-producing carbohydrates. She had given herself the suggestion several times that these foods would satisfy her and would soon make her slim and attractive. Here is the record of her food intake for that 24-hour period one week later:

Tuesday 6:00 P.M.: Half grapefruit; black coffee.

Tuesday 8:30 P.M.: Half grapefruit; cup of consomme; ¾ pound of broiled steak; 1 cup cooked cabbage with butter; salad with oil; black coffee.

Tuesday 11:00 P.M.: 1 ounce of Camembert cheese and a glass of milk.

Wednesday 9:30 A.M.: Slice of honeydew melon; two eggs, scrambled with butter; black coffee.

Wednesday 1:00 P.M.: Cup of consomme; ¼ cold chicken; salad with oil; slice of watermelon; black coffee.

Wednesday 5:00 P.M.: Chopped chicken liver and salad.

Quite a change. In fact, it has all the elements of a stringent, well-disciplined diet. But there were these ingredients of a well-disciplined diet missing: no sacrifice, no deprivation, no hunger, no pills, no irritability, no effort, no discipline. In fact, she apologized for being such a glutton. She was then handed the record of food intake in her own handwriting of the week before that she had mailed in. She got half way through it and had to stop. "Revolting," she said as she handed it back. She got on the scale. It read 171—down three pounds.

As you read her new bill of fare, you may feel pangs of despair as you visualize yourself giving up all the favorite goodies that now delight you. These are the same pangs of despair that you experienced when you looked over the typewritten diet sheets that you resolved to follow the last time you girded your willpower and bludgeoned yourself into a period of denial.

Forget it. Despair not. There is no denial. Everything you crave, you can eat. All that changes is the nature of your craving, and even this happens by itself without your even knowing that it is happening. It happens because you relax deeply and tell *yourself* the truth about carbohydrates.

The auto-genic method of self-relaxation

In reading about various accepted methods for inducing deep relaxation, you will find that some leave you cold, others are fascinating, even beguiling. That feeling of fascination is a clue to its being the right one for you.

In trying the method or methods that attract you, use each period of relaxation that you achieve to visualize yourself going even deeper next time. Use it also to visualize pie, cake, potatoes, spaghetti and other starchy foods as turning into unwanted fat as described in the last chapter. Finally, end each session with thoughts of renewed awareness, alertness, vigor and energy.

Remember, too, that should any emergency arise you will be fully aware of it. The deep relaxation does not take this awareness from you. Your hearing, smell, sight, will be keenly on the alert without conscious effort while you are in a relaxed state. You will always be able to think and have full command of yourself no matter how deep your state.

A well-known German psychiatrist, J. H. Schultz, developed a method of auto-hypnosis that has attained wide popularity in Europe starting in the 1940's. It is called the auto-genic method of self-relaxation.[1]

Schultz defined his method as a series of mental exercises or gymnastics aimed at developing one's capacity for attaining inner relaxation and introspection. He taught the method to his patients as a self-directed way to rid the body of malfunction and to strengthen its healthy potentials. He found that through its use, his patients gained the ability to rest and restore energy; to lose inner tensions; to lessen and even abolish certain pain; to gain control over such otherwise involuntary bodily functions as circulation and metabolism; to increase memory; to accept visualized instructions in the manner of post-hypnotic suggestion.

Schultz recommends that the exercises be performed in a relaxed sitting position, preferably in a comfortable arm chair. Close your eyes and say "I am completely relaxed." Next say,

---

1 *Vebungsheft für das Autogene Training*, 6th ed., (Stuttgart: George Thieme Publishing House, 1947).

"My right arm is completely heavy." (If you are left handed, use your left arm). After about two minutes of concentrating on the growing heaviness of your arm, you are ready to visualize disgusting fat of carbohydrate and the ease of relaxing next time. To terminate the session you concentrate on three suggestions: "The arm is stiff;" "I breathe deeply;" "I open my eyes."

Schultz noted that, if the exercise is done two or three times a day, in one or two weeks the heaviness sensation will be felt in both arms and then in both legs. He recognized the similarity with his method and yoga, a method of progressive relaxation used widely in India and the Far East.

The Schultz method is certainly a simple one and easy to try out with no long succession of steps to memorize. No special deepening techniques were prescribed by Schultz other than the deepening that comes with each successive practice session. If you would like to try this method, check the page, and come back to it again before you are ready to put the book down.

The recorded voice

A recording of trance-inducing suggestions can be a very effective device to speed you on your way to deep relaxation. You can either make your own recording, or purchase one from any number of firms. If you are making your own, tape recorders are the easiest to use. You can experiment with different monologues just by re-recording on the same tapes. Here is one you could use in a prone position. This position has not been used in our previous exercises because one is prone to fall asleep. However, the recorded voice can be used to stop the subject short of sleep, while still sinking to a deep relaxed state. The recorded voice would say:

Take a deep breath. Exhale. Take another deep breath. Exhale. With the third breath you feel a heaviness come over you. Your toes, soles, ankles feel heavy and relaxed. Your lower legs, calves and shins let go in comfortable relaxation. Knees are loose and comfortable. Thighs are heavy, very heavy. Your hips and buttocks sink heavily into the floor. The waist untenses. The back lets go. Your upper torso, chest and neck are relaxed. The space between your shoulders is reached by this wave of relaxation; you feel your very organs functioning harmoniously, in this relaxed state. Even your arms, wrists, fingers are engulfed in this wave of relaxed serenity. Neck muscles and throat are relaxed. Your eyes, jaw, and chin find their relaxed position, making your mouth, tongue and teeth free of tension and perfectly, naturally, comfortable.

Inhale deeply. You feel too heavy to move, too heavy even to keep your eyelids open. They close. With eyes closed, you see a heavy cloud of darkness. It envelops your thoughts. It is different from sleep. It is total quiet of the conscious mind. In this state you hear every word that is being said. You are able to visualize what is asked of you. You are anxious to see the images that will one day become true. The image of yourself standing erect and healthy, many pounds lighter. There, you can see that image now. This is the way you will be. You are already starting to be that attractive image. The only obstacle to reaching your slender, natural self are the carbohydrates that permeate the "stop" foods. You no longer feel attracted to these foods. They turn to the fat that you no longer want. Instead, you will enjoy the "go" foods that are brimming with the vitamins, minerals, proteins necessary for the good health of your body.

The next time that you hear this voice, you will find it easy to relax even more deeply and serenely. Now you will slowly and gradually arouse yourself. You feel full of energy and good spirits. Now you are wide awake!

If you cut this record or tape it, avoid sudden inflections to your voice. Instead, use a steady, forceful monotone that induces relaxation by its sheer droning boredom. Perhaps you will find the voice of a member or friend of the family less distracting than the novelty of your voice talking to you. Inflection should be used only for the purpose of emphasizing the dictatorial firmness of the suggestions.

Turning on the device can be accomplished by an automatic timer which will thus enable you to go through the ritual of getting comfortable and centering down your thoughts for best receptivity of the message.

The message can be changed to suit your own personality. Suggestions can be tailored to your progress, cutting or increasing on quantity or types of food as your progress chart indicates.

A Jesuit priest, a student counselor at St. Louis University, uses hypnotic suggestion to help students through examination periods. Rev. John J. Higgins' soothing treatment of relaxation and concentration became so successful and in such demand that he put it on two sides of a long-playing record. It is now helping students in grade and high schools as well. Nuns have the students listen to Father Higgins' recorded voice three times a day between his visits. They find it improves grades and class behavior.

The Rhodes method

There is a simple "eye closure" method used successfully in auto-hypnosis that is known as the Rhodes technique.[2] It is done in the count of three, seated in a comfortable chair as follows:

As you say "one," out loud, think of your eyelids getting very heavy. As they actually begin to get that heavy feeling, say "two," and think of your eyelids so heavy that they gradually close by themselves. Now, with your eyes shut, say "three"

[2] R. H. Rhodes, *Therapy Through Hypnosis* (New York: Citadel Press, 1952).

and visualize them so tightly shut that you cannot open them no matter how hard you try.

You may now give yourself the anti-carbohydrate suggestions, the visual image of yourself slim, and finally the suggestion that the next time your relaxation will be deeper. At the word, "open," which you can exclaim aloud or mentally, your eyes open and you feel wide awake and refreshed.

The success of this method will depend on how good you are at holding your bounding thoughts in tight rein and keeping them in sharp focus on each idea. This is difficult. It takes practice. Try this method two or three times before judging it.

Should you find this eye closure technique useful, you can gradually eliminate speaking the count aloud, and instead just think one, two, and three. With practice the whole procedure can become almost instantaneous. You sit comfortably, close your eyes and think the number three thought. Immediately, *you* are ready, open, and receptive to slenderizing suggestions.

The Weitzenhoffer technique

The pendulum experiment you tried in Chapter 2 and the relaxation techniques just described are part of an hour-long procedure for attaining deep relaxation preferred by Dr. André M. Weitzenhoffer of Stanford University.[3]

First do the pendulum test, changing its direction many times and in many ways.

Next seat yourself comfortably in a chair and do the hand heaviness technique described earlier in this chapter, with the heaviness transferred to the other arm, both legs and the entire body. You end up by doing Rhodes' eyelid closing technique just described.

Dr. Weitzenhoffer recommends long practice sessions, as much as two hours daily. He also recommends liberal use of

---

3 André M. Weitzenhoffer, Ph.D., *General Techniques of Hypnosis* (New York and London: Grune & Stratton, 1957).

posthypnotic suggestions which will bring about faster induction and deeper states on successive tries.

Use the method which is best for you

Thus, you see how one method borrows from the other and how all can lend themselves to a combination. There is no judge of the best, but yourself. There is no gauge more valid then your own success.

If that success already came with the author's methods introduced earlier in this book, there is no need to change. Possibly some parts of these outside methods might be used to increase that success.

On the other hand, if you are not convinced that the author's methods are doing the most for you in attaining deep relaxation, try one of these other methods. Pick the one that appeals to you. Practice it a number of times, always using your suggestions for inhibiting the intake of pies, cakes, spaghettis, potatoes and other carbohydrate foods. Follow with the visual image of yourself slim, energetic and attractive. And close with suggestions of even deeper trance attainment the next time around. Termination should always include positive statements of "I now feel wide awake, vigorous, and healthier."

Practice sessions should always be in a quiet room where you can concentrate and where you have a reasonable chance of being uninterrupted. Your attitude should be serious, anxious and expectant. Give it your all. There is much at stake, and vast rewards are just minutes away.

Harness time to help you

Should all of these methods fail to provide you with a quick, effective way to relax, there is still an infallible way yet open to you. It is open to every one. It has, in fact, never failed anyone. To give it a name would be to limit and restrain it. It requires freedom and time. So it shall go nameless and so, too, shall it arrive by itself, unannounced, when the time is right. Read about it now, but don't try it, don't force it. Let it try you.

Your desire to attain a trance-like state has already set certain mental wheels in motion. These are the same wheels that permit you to drive your car from home to office without once thinking about the turns you must make, the same wheels that figure out an answer while you sleep on a problem, and the same wheels that deliver up a forgotten name as soon as you stop trying to remember it.

This subconscious mechanism will similarly deliver to you the moments of wonderful, deep relaxation for which you yearn, and during which you can change your life.

All you need to do is stop trying various techniques and give yourself time—quiet time. Spend this time sitting or lying comfortably, idly. It can be at your desk, on your sofa. You might let your thoughts wander on the subject of your losing weight. You might daydream about the clothes you can wear when you are slim, the attractive person you will be. You might meditate on the whole idea of self-mastery through talking to *yourself;* on the many wonderful ways you can improve your life; on the miracle of the mind.

You will not recognize that anything has happened when it does happen. You will feel that time has flown and what appeared to be only 15 minutes of reverie was in reality 45 minutes. That is a sure sign that it has happened. Your subconscious has delivered up a completely relaxed state just as you ordered. To repeat it, you go to the same chair or sofa, under the same relaxed conditions, with the same lack of concern about the method. You muse over the same matters that you did before, letting your thoughts gradually turn to the business at hand: "The pie is really fat. I feel it dripping disgustingly down my throat, sticking as unwanted flesh to my ribs. I see myself turning from such carbohydrate "stop" foods and instead thriving on such "go" desserts as melon and grapefruit."

The latent forces of your inner self can even take over the function of suggestion. Meditation and contemplation of a problem have a way of setting off the process of solution, even if that solution means a change in our own inner conditioning attitudes. How or why this happens can probably be better explained from philosophical or spiritual approaches rather than psychological. It may be said to be the workings of a superconscious rather than the subconscious.

Rev. Charlie W. Shedd, author of *Pray Your Weight Away,*[4] calls it divine assistance. He lost 100 pounds in three years by devoting his quiet time to direct prayer—prayer for understanding of why he overate, as well as prayer for assistance in eating the right food.

That this works in our everyday lives is quite evident, not exclusively of divine origin, but just as often with origins of fear and anxiety. Quiet time spent in negative worry will, in due course, affect our very appearance and our health. We are what we think, and our thoughts within ourselves are much more powerful than noisy surface thoughts. You can turn these quiet thoughts into powerful reconditioners that will silently reshape your eating habits in the direction you want.

Your quiet time may also take place simultaneously with the reading of this book. Your self-therapy sessions may take place in their own good time after you read the book through.

Just as there are people of every description, so are there limitless numbers of ways that people think, react, behave. Many readers have already practiced relaxation right from Chapter 1, and by now have acquired a high degree of skill in attaining deep states of relaxation. Others were sparked later in the book to dynamic and sudden action. They may have already caught up to early starters. Many have not yet

---

4 (Philadelphia: Lippincott, 1957).

chosen to try the early relaxation monologues or any of the subsequent techniques. There is no reason to force the issue. If you have been motivated to begin, fine. If you have not, pick your own time, and do so with the assurance that every page read in your quiet time is going to bat for you and will support your effort when you make your move.

The time has come to take a long hard look at food so that our listening, receptive and somewhat exposed subconscious can now be given the information it needs to guide the appetite along healthful, thinning lines.

REVIEW

The only infallible way to choose the right method is to try them all. Grade each one by the depth of trance-like relaxation you reach through it. Skip any that does not appeal to you. Be sure, also, to try some quiet time described on page 112.

9

CREATING YOUR LIST OF
"STOP" AND "GO" FOODS

You are now about to create a list of healthful "go" foods for yourself. When you have it, all you will have to do is hold it in your hand when you talk to *yourself*.

There will be no need to wrestle with yourself about talking yourself out of some particular favorite dish. All you have to do while you read this chapter is to accept the fact that carbohydrates turn to fat—the same fat that detracts from appearance, brings premature old age, and causes day to day unhappiness.

If we can classify foods by their carbohydrate content, it will then be possible to put an automatic taboo on the high carbohydrate content "stop" foods and an automatic blessing on the low carbohydrate "go" foods. There will be foods you now like and dislike in each category. Later, you will like all the "go" foods and dislike all the "stop" foods. You will be reeducating your taste buds in just a few minutes of self-hypnotic suggestions. Then, as the pounds drop away, you will rejoice in your new eating ways. Your enjoyment of eating will increase, not lessen. Instead of guilt lurking behind every forkful of starch or sweet, you will eat lustily with a free conscience, enjoying meals with family and friends, at home or in restaurants, and savoring them as you never have before.

Why carbohydrates are condemned

Carbohydrates are about to get the axe. This purveyor of poundage, this killer in sweets clothing, is guilty of murder. It must go. But first it must be apprehended and identified. What is a carbohydrate and how do we recognize it? If you were a chemist, you would know it to contain carbon, hydrogen and oxygen. These are the same elements in fat, also used as a fuel by the body. In fact, as we all know, carbohydrates are easily translated into fat for storage by the body. The two most common families of carbohydrates are the starches and the sugars, both closely related chemically and both used as fuel by the body. The process of digestion converts starch to sugar. Our manufacturing processes can do likewise; cornstarch is made into corn syrup. Yet we constantly add sugar to starch when we eat. Cereals, cakes, cookies would be tasteless without sugar. Carbohydrate begets fat.

Sugar and starch are both delivered by the alimentary canal to the bloodstream as simple sugars. Sugar is habit forming. It creates an appetite for itself, not for other foods. In fact it dulls your appetite for other foods. The person who eats a piece of candy reaches for another. Children become undernourished when they are exposed to excessive sweets.

The medical profession now recognizes the carbohydrate for the villain that it is. Doctors realize that weight gain comes not only from the high calorie content of carbohydrate foods, but from the tendency of carbohydrates to change the body chemistry. High carbohydrate fare puts on weight faster than equal caloried high protein fare. A person might lose weight on a 2800 calorie diet of proteins and fats, but a 2800 calorie diet of starches and sweets may put weight on that same person.

The theory has been advanced that carbohydrates affect the ability of the body to convert calories into energy. Sweets and starches, in other words, slow up the metabolic rate. Besides adding calories, they subtract from the body's ability to burn up these calories. Thus carbohydrates provide a sort of double action weight gain.

Proteins on the other hand provide a double action weight loss. Relatively low in calories, they also step up the metabolic rate that burns up calories. It is a little publicized fact that one gram of pure protein has more calories of fuel than one gram of pure carbohydrate—5.65 calories for the protein, 4.1 calories for the carbohydrate. But the body does not treat protein as fuel. It is too valuable as building material to burn. It keeps the furnace in repair so that it can burn fats and carbohydrates more effectively. Excess protein in the diet is excreted rather than stored as the body stores fats and carbohydrates.

Unfortunately, fattening carbohydrates are cheap. Slenderizing proteins are expensive. This has been a contributing cause to the ease and readiness with which we have become used to tossing potato chips, pretzels and other packaged (carbohydrate) snacks into our systems. Proteins are usually confined to dinner, our most expensive meal of the day, when the main course includes meat, fish or poultry. Breakfasts are notoriously carbohydrate—heavy and inexpensive with dry cereals, doughnuts and danish pastry the typical fatteners. It is apparent that our desire to save time as well as money has led us off the path of proper eating. Carbohydrate foods lend themselves to ready-to-eat forms such as cakes, cookies, candies. Proteins usually require on-the-spot preparation.

Why proteins are praised

The ironic fact is that we get our full money's worth of nourishment with the more expensive proteins. Whereas, cheap as they are, the carbohydrates provide less nourishment for the dollar. Our entire body is made mostly of protein from the skin and muscles right through to the bones. Protein-

starved bodies sag and bulge. Bodies well nourished with protein are firm and erect.

Our hair, nails and internal organs all need protein to keep
in repair. Brittle hair or nails is a sign of protein deficiency.
Both take on new resiliency when protein is restored in proper
abundance to the body.

Even the time-saving aspect of carbohydrates is an illusion.
For even more quickly than they are eaten does their energy-
producing value disappear. The quick lift of pastries and
coffee is followed by a sharp drop in energy. It provides a
charge of blood sugar for instant energy, but tests show that
needed blood sugar is once again in low supply before the
morning gets under way. Pancakes and syrup, waffles and syrup, french toast and syrup—all are carbohydrate-heavy. They
contain starches that turn into sugar when digested and pour
into the blood stream. The pancreas, whose job is to produce
the insulin that aids in the storage of sugar, works overtime
after such a breakfast. Over-stimulated, it produces so much
insulin that the bloodstream is soon deprived of its sugar so
necessary for energy and brain efficiency. So, what starts out
as a feast of blood-sugar usually turns into a blood-sugar fa-
mine soon after you arrive at the office.

Time spent in cooking eggs or bacon pays off ten-fold in
energy-time gained. Proteins provide lasting power. A small
amount of carbohydrate, taken with protein, trickles into the
bloodstream for hours. Digestion takes longer. Metabolism is
faster and energy levels are higher.

But you must have a balanced diet

Carbohydrates may be criticized as food, but we cannot do
without them completely. Proteins may be the true staff of
life, not those loaves of carbohydrate, but we cannot live on
protein alone. The body needs some fat and sugar to produce
body heat and energy. It needs vitamins and minerals found
in a variety of foods. In short, the body needs a balanced diet.

If we were to condition ourselves to abstain totally from carbohydrates, there would be hardly any foods we could eat. All fruits and vegetables have some carbohydrate content. So do dairy products, grains, and nuts. Most fish and meats have only a trace of carbohydrate, but it's there. Poultry comes closest to being entirely free of carbohydrate.

Our body needs carbohydrates. There is no need to shun them. It needs them in the quantity that nature supplies them in most fruits and vegetables. It does not need them in the tidal wave of sugar- and starch-rich foods which we have adopted as a way of life, but which in reality is a way of death.

Our body needs minerals. Our teeth and bones need calcium, our blood needs iron. In 1873 a German chemist fed dogs and pigeons a diet of pure carbohydrates, proteins and fats that were free of mineral salts. They all died within a few weeks. Some years later science fully established the importance of various mineral elements in the maintenance of life. Today, with our soils greatly depleted of minerals, farmers are urged to replace them with proper fertilization, and women who prepare foods are constantly reminded to save pot liquids and use them in sauces and soups. Since minerals dissolve in the water used for cooking vegetables and fruits, the liquids contain these valuable elements—too valuable to throw down the kitchen drain. Fruits and vegetables provide us with the precious minerals we need. Meats and cereals, especially refined cereals, have comparatively little mineral content.

Now you can eat all you want—and lose weight

A man in Huntington, Long Island, recently captured the imagination of overweight persons all over the country when he sailed his yacht out into Huntington Bay, dropped anchor and went on a diet of water, tea and vitamin pills. Despite the temptations offered by fellow yachtsmen who waved food at him, he stuck it out for 21 days under the watchful eye of his physician, and lost 30 pounds, consuming his own fat away from 245 pounds down to 215 pounds.

The fasting undoubtedly did this man a world of good. However, it is not a permanent solution. If he could acquire effortlessly and overnight—as through self-hypnosis—the ability to eat the right foods, he could eat all he wanted and still lose weight.

"Eat all I want and still lose weight?" That's right. "But what about calories?" Yes, calories do add up when you eat quantity, but they do not add up very fast with low-carbohydrate foods. Furthermore, high protein foods stay with you longer, extending your satisfied feeling without extending your waistline. So, chances are good you will not want more food than your body will utilize. Self-hypnosis is already helping you to overcome habitual overeating, and will soon restore your eating to normal, quantitatively. It is the *qualitative* aspect that needs the most correction.

The Huntington yachtsman found this out soon after he returned to shore. He continued to lose weight gradually for several weeks, just because he had not fully returned to his old eating habits. But it was inevitable that, without auto-conditioning, these habits would return. And return they did, together with much of the poundage he had lost. Six months later he had climbed back up from 212 to 220 and was resolving (there's built-in trouble right there) to hold it at 220.

Although the matter is still quite controversial, the idea that slimming depends solely on eating less calories is now on the way out. It is not calories, but the *kind* of calories that counts. Eat the *right kind* of calories and you can eat as much as you may be eating now in carbohydrates, and lose weight instead of gain.

How to select your favorite foods

In order to recondition yourself to avoid high carbohydrate foods and to be attracted to meats and other high protein foods instead, it is necessary for you to make the choice yourself. There are only two rules to which you must conform:

1. You must limit carbohydrate-heavy foods.
2. You must select balanced, diversified foods.

To help you with the first, tables of carbohydrate content for most foods are provided on pages 187-223. To help you with the second, your physician may be consulted, or you may find complete safety in numbers, that is, there is no risk in changing your diet, if you do not limit it severely, but instead adopt a large number of foods that you have enjoyed in the past:

Do you like sirloin steak, roast leg of lamb, broiled chicken, lamb chops, pork chops, wiener schnitzel? Do your favorite fish dishes include broiled cod, swordfish, haddock, halibut? Or steamed clams, oysters on the half shell, broiled lobster, cooked crabmeat? What are your favorite vegetables? Fresh asparagus, braised celery, boiled cabbage, brussel sprouts, spinach, tomatoes, turnips—all seasoned just the way you like? These are all in your future.

Also in your future are gourmet cheeses such as Gruyère, Cheddar, and Parmesan; sophisticated soufflés and omelets; exotic mousses and aspics; and crisp, interesting salads to your heart's content.

You can enjoy a second and a third portion of shish kebab, but not one sliver of pie. You can revel in corned beef and cabbage, but no boiled potatoes. Your swordfish steaks can be an inch thick, but not one inch of crêpes suzette.

High carbohydrate foods—poison to the image of our true, slender self—get blackballed. They will go on a "stop" list. This is the list you have already started to lose your taste for, because it is the taste of disgusting fat itself.

Foods with a moderate amount of carbohydrate content do not belong on our "stop" list, nor do they belong on our "go" list. Borrowing from the traffic specialists, they belonged on a "caution" list. These are eaten only when it is expedient.

They are not in the eat-all-you-want "go" category, nor are they taboo. Treat these like you used to when you were a child and unexpected company came to dinner. Mother would call out "FHB." Everybody knew that meant "Family hold back."

There is a thrilling amount of low carbohydrate foods on the "go" list. It is by far the largest list of all. There are even more you can list, as it is not complete. Add any items of poultry, fish, or meat that you wish. Only the most ordinarily accepted and popular items are listed. It would render the list less practical to include such rarities as goose, whale steak, venison, and the like. These are all excellent low carbohydrate, high protein foods and obtainable in many stores, but relatively few persons have even tasted them as compared to those who dine on chopped steak and chicken.

How to recognize "stop" foods (See Table, p. 125)

Ordinary white and rye breads and rolls are public enemy number one to persons who are overweight. They and their partners in crime, cakes and pies, head the "stop" list. Similar baked goods such as doughnuts, pastry, biscuits, muffins, pancakes, waffles, crackers, cookies, tarts, éclairs, all replete with fatty carbohydrates, are strictly "stop." Spaghetti and macaroni products are practically pure starch and that means practically pure human fat. With them on the "stop" list are other Italian pastas such as lasagna, ravioli. Noodles are "stop." Alphabet soup spells trouble. All breakfast cereals, hot or cold, are too heavily carbohydrate. So is rice. Sauces and gravies thickened with cornstarch or flour are taboo.

Sweets are out without exception: candy, ice cream, sugar, sweet drinks, soda. Jellies, jams, and preserves are too sugarfull. Don't put gelatin in this category, though; it is on the "go" list. The test for liquor, wine, and liqueur is the taste. If it is sweet, it is carbohydrate-heavy. Beer is banned. Undoubtedly, you feel some pangs of remorse about giving up some of these old favorites. You must remind yourself at this time of the miracle of self-hypnosis. There is no "giving up." The "stop" foods actually give you up. Practically overnight you pass them by because you no longer want them.

A few fruits and vegetables are on the "stop" list. You already know about potatoes, and of course sweet potatoes are no less starchy than white varieties. An ear of corn has nearly as much carbohydrate as an average size potato. Pulpy beans such as limas and kidneys or the dried varieties are bulging with carbohydrate. The slim variety, on the other hand, like string beans, are on the slimming "go" list. Heading the carbohydrate-heavy fruits are dates, with bananas a close second.

The "stop" list is actually a very unimpressive list of scoundrels. Line them up together on the kitchen table, free of their colorful wrappings. Pile them up alongside one another: a heap of sugar, a bundle of noodles, a drift of flour—devoid of the glamorous commercials and tempting shapes that you may have become "hooked" on—and you have a sickly-looking mess that you would never want to have dissolved in your blood stream or stored around your waist. What a relief it will be to be rid of them. A load off you. You almost feel lighter already!

Recognizing "caution" foods (See Table, p. 125)

Nature provides us with enough carbohydrates in fruits, vegetables, and berries to give our bodies the fuel to meet its current needs for energy. There are plenty of these on the "go" list of foods. There are also animal fats. And there is also our own fat.

If you want to burn off some of your own fat, it is necessary to eliminate some of nature's more generous portions of energy-giving foods. Once you have reached the weight you want, these "caution" foods can go back on your eating schedule. However, you will not be able to eat all you want of them, as you will the "go" foods, without risk of converting some to fat.

"Caution" foods consist of more of the pulpy vegetables such as carrots, peas and some varieties of squash. Pumpkins are in this category. Most of our common eating fruits such as apples, pears, and grapes have just enough carbohydrate to warrant a go easy attitude on the part of weight-conscious persons.

Other "caution" foods include most of the common eating nuts such as walnuts, almonds, and pecans. Go easy on blackberries, raspberries, and their cousins.

Chances are you will want to begin your weight loss with a gratifying measure of success and will choose to start by placing "caution" foods off limits. This will simplify talking yourself thin. You will be able to hold your "go" food list in your hand and concentrate your thoughts and imagery on this one entity. Later, as you reach your desired weight, you can add "caution" foods to this same list, cautiously and avoid juggling two lists.

Enjoying "go" foods (See Table, p. 126)

Here comes the most tempting array of foods. And it is open season. Eat all you want of the foods on your "go" list. They are high in protein, low in carbohydrate, and contain all the minerals and vitamins your body needs when consumed in normal quantity and diversification.

All cuts of beef and lamb are "go." The so-called organ meats—liver, heart, brain, sweetbreads, kidney, tongue—are all A-Okay. Roast pork, ham, and veal are fine. Sausages, frankfurters, bologna, and other packaged pure meats are good. Roast duck, chicken, and other fowl are excellent.

"STOP" FOODS

Vegetables

Beans (dried and lima)
Beets
Corn (fresh or canned)
Parsnips
Potatoes (white or sweet)

Fruits and Nuts

Apricots
Bananas
Dates

Miscellaneous Foods

Breakfast cereals
  (dried or cooked)
Bread, rolls, crackers
Macaroni, noodles, spaghetti,
  and rice
Jams, jellies, and preserves
Ice cream, candy, cakes, pies

Sauces and gravies thickened
  with flour or cornstarch
Beer
Sweet wines and liqueurs
Soda
Sugar (and all sweetening
  agents containing sorbitol)

"CAUTION" FOODS

Meat and Poultry

Bologna
Corned beef hash
Canned luncheon meat
Frankfurters
Sausage

Dairy Products

Butter
Cream
Mayonnaise

Vegetables

Carrots
Peas (fresh or canned)
Pumpkin
Rutabagas
Squash (winter, zucchini)

Fruits and Nuts

Apples (fresh or cooked)
Blackberries
Cherries
Figs
Grapes
Oranges
Orange juice
Peaches
Pineapple

Plums
Raspberries
Strawberries
Almonds
Brazil nuts
Coconut
Peanuts
Pecans
Walnuts

"GO" FOODS

Meat and Poultry

Bacon
Beef, cooked or dried, all cuts
　(chuck, hamburger, sirloin)
Beef (canned),
　corned
Brains
Kidneys, beef, veal
Lamb, roast or chops
　(grilled or broiled)
Liver, beef

Pork, roast or chops
　(grilled or broiled)
Chicken (roasted, broiled,
　or stewed)
Duck (roasted)
Turkey (roasted)
Ham (baked or boiled)
Heart, beef
Sweetbreads
Tongue
Veal cutlet, chops, roast

Fish and Seafood

Clams (raw or steamed)
Cod
Crab Meat
Flounder ⎫
Haddock ⎬ baked or broiled
Halibut ⎪
Herring ⎭
Lobster (boiled or broiled)
Mackerel (boiled, baked, or
　broiled)

Mussels (raw or steamed)
Oysters (raw or in a stew)
Salmon (fresh or canned)
Sardines (canned, drain oil
　from can)
Scallops
Shad (baked)
Shrimp (boiled)
Swordfish (baked or broiled)
Trout (baked or broiled)

Dairy Products

Cheese:
  Cheddar
  Cottage
  Gorgonzola
  Gruyère
  Parmesan
  Blue
  Swiss

Eggs:
  prepared in any way

Milk:
  or milk beverages *

* Should be limited to one glass daily.

Vegetables and Fruits

Asparagus
Beans (green, string, or wax)
Broccoli
Brussels sprouts
Cabbage
Cauliflower
Celery (raw or cooked)
Cucumber
Eggplant
Endive
Escarole
Kale
Kohlrabi

Lettuce
Mushrooms
Okra
Onions
Parsley
Peppers (green and red)
Radishes
Sauerkraut
Spinach
Squash (summer)
Tomatoes (cooked or fresh)
Turnips (white or yellow)
Water cress

Fruits

Grapefruit
Lemons
Melons (all varieties)
Rhubarb (stewed)
Tangerines

What about bacon and other high-in-fat meats? They are on the "go" list, too. There are three to four times as many lean meats on the "go" list as fat meats. This is the proper proportion to maintain when you plan your meals. If you selected at random without planning, the law of averages would automatically keep this three or four to one lean-fat ratio. It is the same ratio that the body consumes its own reserves.

Most fish is splendid protein food. This includes halibut, mackerel, salmon, haddock, flounder, trout, and all of the other popular varieties. The shellfish are no exception: oysters, mussels, clams, crabs, lobsters and shrimp. Even the canned fish are fine, and, since mayonnaise is "caution," all sorts of fish salads and fish recipes no doubt come to mind.

Speaking of salads, you can have an orgy. Lettuce of all types, cucumbers, tomatoes, celery, green or red peppers, onions, water cress, radishes—all are very much "go." In addition, you will see on the list such delicious vegetables as broccoli, turnips, kale, cauliflower, string beans, spinach, cabbage, brussel sprouts, and a score of others.

Another wide range of good eating and all you want of it is in the dairy products. Only milk itself needs to be taken in proportion to the place it has on the list. A glass a day, or its equivalent used in cooking is "go." Eat all the eggs and cheese you want.

In planning recipes, avoid adding flour, wine, and other ingredients that are not on the "go" list. Use cooking oils and fats in moderation. Butter, lard, and margarine are high in calories, so take care. And, as mentioned before, mayonnaise gets the "caution" light.

Grapefruit, oranges, melon and rhubarb are on the "go" list. Lemons and lemon juice may be used freely in cooking. Desserts as you have known them will be the largest single change in your eating habits. But, remember, no painful disciplinary adjustment is necessary. All you need do is discipline yourself into a comfortable chair, review the relaxation instructions already given and follow the suggestion instructions that are about to be given.

Food can be like money in the bank

"Go" foods are brimming with healthful nutrition. They are packed with all your body needs to maintain itself on a high level of resistance to disease, to revitalize itself from inside to out, and to serve you efficiently as a dynamo of heat, brainpower and energy.

We are certain that the body, which cannot store protein as it does carbohydrate and fat, will have an ample, steady supply of these valuable building blocks. Minerals and vitamins abound in the fruits and vegetables. Besides its calcium, milk and milk products are significant sources of vitamin A and riboflavin, essential in the development of new tissue. Fish livers are another source of vitamin A, or fortified margarine may be used.

Vitamin C, or ascorbic acid, is liberally provided by the "go" citrus fruits. Thiamine and iron are found in pork notably, but also in other meats and vegetables.

In short, all essentials, plus many more benefits, are in your "go" foods.

Your own "go" list

Your next step in talking yourself thin is to copy the list of "go" foods on a piece of paper. *Do not tear it from the book.* The reason for going through the process of writing out the list is so your subconscious knows what is on it. You do not have to memorize it. The process of writing it once is enough.

Later you will hold this list you have written and refer to it in your auto-suggestions. You will not even have to look at it. *You* will know just what you mean when reference is made to the list, after you have written it once.

There is another important reason for writing out the list. By so doing you are giving your consent. You will be able to tell *yourself* that this is a list of foods to which you have agreed. This consent is vital if your subconscious is to go to work for you. If you have any reservation about giving *your-self* this consent, let your physician look the list over and give you his approval. You must feel "go" about your "go" foods.

It will help, as always, to visualize as you write, rather than to do a mechanical copy job. If you are writing chopped steak, visualize how you like to prepare it. Do you chop onions for it? Prepare mushrooms? Or both? Picture each food just the way you enjoy it most. Think of when or where you had it last and how good it tasted.

You do not copy the "stop" foods. They are no longer in the picture. The only list you need is the "go" list. Later you will add some of the "caution" foods to your "go" list or take some further action to restore them to your food consumption. Meanwhile, to drop weight significantly, abstain from "caution" foods as much as possible.

Right now is the time to copy your "go" list, for in the next chapter, you will use it to bring about the most astounding miracle of your lifetime.

REVIEW

Write out your "Go" list. Visualize each food, just the way you like it, as you put it on the list, copying from page 126. You may read over the "caution" list but don't copy it. Read the foods on the "stop" list. Kiss them good riddance.

10

FOOD CONDITIONING YOURSELF FOR EASIER WEIGHT LOSS

By now you have acquired two major essentials of the talk yourself thin process: the ability to place yourself in a deep trance-like state of relaxation; and a balanced diet of high protein foods. This chapter will provide you with the third essential that will enable you to cause your weight to take a nose-dive. That essential is the technique for etching your "go" list of foods on *yourself* as a new permanent healthful way of eating.

If you stop right here, and decide instead to use your "go" list as a new diet—one you will follow faithfully—forget it. Do not even bother. It will be a waste of time for your waistline. One year from now it will measure the same or more. You will have remained on that treadmill of going on a diet and getting off it, of getting some poundage off and watching it go back on again. You will have exerted a tremendous amount of will power—again—and lost.

The miracle of hypnosis is now yours to use. It gets you off the diet treadmill. It breaks the old eating habits which have made you what you are today, and substitutes new weight-losing habits in their place. You need to use no willpower. It just happens. You become a person who naturally eats right and looks right.

Prepare for effective therapy

It is now time to return to that comfortable arm chair that you use to practice relaxation. You will use your favorite method for attaining a deep trance-like state of bliss. If you have not developed a preference for any described in Chapter 8, it is recommended that you use the simple elevator technique described earlier on pages 90-92, applying the countdown to hasten the deepening powers. It will be the same as your previous sessions—the countdown, the suggestions, the return—only this time something new will be added: your "go" list of nutritious foods.

Place the "go" list on a table in front of you or to the side, within easy grasp. It may be open or folded closed, whichever is more convenient. It is preferable for this paper to be the only object on the table.

Take the book with you, be seated comfortably and read on. You will be given a lengthy monologue similar to the first relaxation technique. This monologue can be put into your own words after the sequence of ideas is clear to you. It will form the core of your slenderizing suggestions. You will be changing the words and perhaps adding other accelerating techniques later, but you will do well to consider this monologue as the keystone of your self-hypnosis.

Your food conditioning monologue

Is the room quiet? Can you foresee any interruptions? Is there a periodic noise of some sort in the distance? If so, are you prepared to use it to deepen your hypnosis as an aid rather than a hindrance? With all in readiness, read the monologue that follows. Review the main stream of its suggestive thought, outlined for you at the close. Then proceed to relax, follow that thought, and emerge—energetic and gustatorially renewed.

I am deeply relaxed. As I breathe slowly and deeply I begin to feel the presence of my body. I can feel the shoes on my feet, my ankles, my legs. I feel the clothes around my thighs, stomach, chest, shoulders. It is an opposite feeling to that of numbness. It is a feeling of extreme sensitivity and awareness of my body. It seems that I can almost feel the skin, the tissues beneath it, and the fat and ugliness that protrudes in unwanted bulges. My whole mind is focused on my body.

I will now project time into the future. It is tomorrow. It is a week from tomorrow, a month from tomorrow. It is now many months from now. I begin to feel what it is like to lose this heavy, unwanted fat. I can visualize myself slender, solid, trim of figure. I look younger. I radiate good health. I move with agility. It seems effortless to be active. I see that I have attained this state quite easily by eating the right foods. It is the "go" list of foods that will take me in time from now to then and to this slender self that I really am. (You pick up "go" list and hold it in your hand.)

From this present time on, I will not crave foods that I have agreed to abolish. Instead I will be perfectly satisfied, both emotionally and bodily, with the selected foods I have agreed to eat and itemized on this "go" list. (Pause about 30-seconds and visualize yourself thoroughly content after a "go" breakfast, arising completely satisfied after a typical "go" lunch or dinner.)

When I am heavy I feel thick, bloated, distorted; just as I feel bloated after a heavy meal. In the future, when I have eaten a normally moderate amount of the foods I have agreed to eat, my mind will tell me "enough." Just a little of this nutritious food will give me the same satisfaction as when I ate more. Under no circumstances will I feel it necessary to eat any of the prohibited foods on the "stop" list. Seldom will

*I find it necessary to eat foods on the "caution" list, but when
I do it will be in extreme moderation.*

*I am completely comforted and self-assured. I recall once
again the slender image that is my true self and hold that
image lovingly in my mind, knowing that I am soon to permanently assume that image, with full satisfaction and without hunger on the way.*

*I am now going to count up from one to ten. I will become
more and more alert and refreshed with every count. The
elevator rises as I count. One ... two ... three ... four ...
Each time I practice this self-hypnosis I will be able to enter
a hypnotic state more easily and comfortably, more deeply
and quickly ... five ... six ... seven ... eight ... nine ...
ten!*

The use of the elevator method of emergence pre-supposes
you have used this method of induction. If you used any other
method of inducing relaxation, you should, of course, use
the technique for awakening from the trance recommended
for that particular method.

Digest the discourse for easy use

This lengthy monologue need not be memorized. You can
capsule the ideas in it for easy remembering, just as you may
have done for the induction monologue in Chapter 8. It is
not even necessary to give the remembered ideas words at all.
You go from idea to idea, holding each in your mind long
enough to consider it thoughtfully and to permit accompany-
ing images their momentary place in your mind's eye.

Here are the pertinent thoughts and images in the "go"
list monologue:

1. I am relaxed and breathing deeply.
2. I am aware of my body, toes to head.
3. I look into the future and see myself thin.
4. I pick up my "go" list of foods.

5. I will be perfectly satisfied with these foods, even in moderation.
6. I will find it unnecessary to eat any "stop" foods.
7. I will eat "caution" foods cautiously.
8. I see myself becoming slender without hunger.
9. My next session will be quicker, deeper.
10. I emerge alert and refreshed.

These ten ideas follow a simple and logical course. They lend themselves to step-by-step mental action. Read them over several times. Then put the book down and see if you can think them.

Once you are able to think these thoughts in order, you are ready to start your first full-dress talk yourself thin session. It should require only five to ten minutes, divided approximately as follows:

First minute: You pull down shades or turn off bright lights, seat yourself comfortably, eliminate any distractions, and quiet your thoughts.

Second minute: You deepen relaxation, using favorite method.

Third minute: You attain a trance-like state and begin to concentrate on your body.

Fourth minute: You visualize yourself slender.

Fifth minute: You pick up "go" list, and visualize your satisfaction with it, and your alienation to the "stop" list.

Sixth minute: You emerge.

The above is not meant to limit you on any of the steps. Take all the time you please. Or hasten a step if you are practiced. Now is the time to memorize the ten ideas and use them in a session. Stop reading here—and begin.

Expect gradual progress

You have completed your first full auto-conditioning session to lose weight. What happens now? Do you rush off to your scale? Sit down and eat? Try another session? Read another chapter?

The answer is you live life just as you always have, do just what you normally feel like doing. Nothing has happened to warrant special attention or change of routine. The better you are able to forget the event, until the next time, the better it will work. It is never a healthy attitude to become self-conscious about yourself. In fact, watching yourself now will prove nothing, because the transformation that has started in you, has started in the subconscious. You cannot be conscious about the subconscious.

A school principal in her middle thirties, asked if she noticed any of these behavior effects in herself after her first hypnosis session, replied, "Not at first. I felt at perfect ease. There was no sense of restriction that I felt so many times before when I embarked on a diet. I had no problems and instead had a strong feeling of well-being. I could watch other people eat all sorts of things and it did not do anything to me. When I automatically passed up dessert, it made me start! Then I laughed when I realized what was happening."

The best way for you to realize what is happening is to see it on your weight progress chart. Suggestions for preparing this were given to you on page 45. Now is the time to get it started. It is from this day on that your weight loss will begin officially, as a self-induced re-conditioning process. Your weight today is the first entry you make at the left side of the chart, unless you have already started it. In that case, the line you have drawn until today is probably horizontal or close to it. It reflects your normal weight pattern, possibly leveled off or sloping slightly downward due both to the conditioning effect of early practice sessions and the suggestive power of the words you are reading.

You will be entering your weight each day with a dot on the chart and connecting the dot to form a line graph of your descending weight. Each vertical step on the graph is one half pound. Since your daily weight loss will probably average less than this, you may go days without any visible drop to the line of the graph. This should not discourage you. The transformation has begun.

Watch your weight tumble

Imperceptible diminishment of your measurements will become dramatic changes in your waistline. Unimpressive ounces trimmed from your weight will add up to significant poundage lost.

The school principal whom we mentioned previously weighed $203\frac{1}{2}$ when she began June 1st. The first three days there was no perceptible change. Then the scale showed $1\frac{1}{2}$ pounds loss, down to 202. By the time the week was over, her chart line, horizontal for three days, had taken a nose-dive to show a loss of three pounds in four days. At the end of one month, she weighed $192\frac{1}{2}$; two months, 185; three months $176\frac{1}{2}$; four months, 171; five months, 168.

Her weight loss tapered off in September and October. She attributed this to the start of school. Apparently, her emotional involvement in her work had something to do with her overeating and wrong eating to begin with. But her new conditioning triumphed. She lost four pounds her sixth month and five pounds her seventh month for a total of 44 pounds lost in that period.

Your own progress will show similar periods of slowing up and renewed acceleration. Day-to-day variations can be due to a number of factors. Variations in bowel activity and in body water content will affect your weight. So will the time of day you weigh yourself. If you have a busy schedule, with a sense of pressure or urgency, your metabolism is stepped up and a few more ounces can be burned off. Particularly strenuous physical or mental activity can also burn off a few ounces and also effect the body water content.

These day-to-day variations are compounded by week-to-week and month-to-month variations. Even the weather can have an effect. Your food intake will vary with emotional stresses and long range changes in your environment.

Controlling your progress

The frequency with which you repeat the self-hypnosis sessions will be one way of controlling your progress. Another way to control your progress is to make your sessions more effective.

How often should you hold a self-hypnosis session? If you are attaining a fairly deep state of relaxation, three times a week to start will be adequate depending on the individual. Then, after a few weeks, you can taper off. If you are not yet adept at attaining deep relaxation, or if your suggestive visualization of the "go" foods' slenderizing effect is not vivid, you may have to hold numerous sessions before you start to lose weight at the rate you want.

To insure prompt success with a minimum of sessions, spaced about a day or so apart, you should review the techniques for attaining deep relaxation covered initially in Chapter 5 and in detail in Chapter 8. Sometimes the significance of information does not strike home the first time around. What may not have seemed important earlier, can now be understood in the framework of the entire process of talking yourself thin. The apparently trifling act of relaxation is now understood as an essential part of the miracle of self-hypnosis.

In each of your relaxation practice sessions, insert the suggestions spelled out in this chapter in place of the short form suggestions previously used. In this way each practice of relaxation will take you closer to your "go" list orientation. In a few practice sessions you will attain a very deep state and remarkable effectiveness for your suggestions, because every practice session contains the suggestion that enables the next to be even more successful.

More telling suggestions

Here are some variations in the "go" list suggestions which will augment your routine. Never lose sight of the main suggestion. "I see myself thin. This 'go' list of foods will nourish me, satisfy me as I grow thin." But add these reinforcements to improve your results.

Suppose you have one particular carbohydrate food item that has steadily proven your downfall. You may not master it in your first few sessions. To sink it, you may have to aim your suggestions at it directly. Suppose the culprit is chocolate. Here is a suggestion to add to the main routine:

I will realize from this point forward that I will have absolutely no desire to eat chocolate. It is on my stop list because it represents to me fat and ugliness. I am talking now particularly to that part of my mind that has been attracted to chocolate and that stimulates my taste buds at the appearance, smell, taste, or thought of chocolate. From now on this part of my mind will consider chocolate no more tasty than the fat it becomes. This part of my mind will know the damage that chocolate can do to my teeth, to my health, and to my appearance.

The "disgusting" approach

Our imagination plays tricks on us. We, too, can play tricks on our imagination. For instance, if we were to imagine ourselves being forced to eat chocolate against our will, bars and bars of it or boxes and boxes, until we became thoroughly sick to our stomach, and if we did a "good job" in that imagining, we would feel a sense of disgust at the next sight of chocolate. If that imagining were to be done while we were in the deep state of relaxation and heightened suggestibility that disgust for chocolate would remain with us for a long time. In fact, it would probably be a long enough time for the habit to be broken and a more healthful, nutritious and nonfattening food substituted in our favorite food's hall of fame.

The technique to use here is simple. Add a minute to your auto-suggestion period, right after you have made suggestions regarding the adequacy of your "go" list. Next, when you visualize the danger of "stop" foods, tell *yourself* that you realize that what you have been doing about chocolate, if consolidated in time, would look like this: then visualize forced feeding *ad nauseam*. Visualize yourself being forced to eat an entire box by somebody you must obey—and then another and another. Go through the motions of chewing it and swallowing it, until you can stand no more. End the suggestion with the anti-chocolate paragraph above.

Another trick on the imagination was described earlier. You can make chocolate taste like burnt rubber or onions, merely by imagining it tasting so while in self-hypnosis. Improvise your own imagery or monologue. If you have never smelled rubber burning, you had better settle for onion-flavored chocolate or some other essence sufficiently distasteful to you to short-circuit your craving and turn it into loathing.

Your monologue might go like this:

I speak now to that portion of my mind that goads me into eating chocolate despite my knowledge that chocolate erodes my teeth, fattens my body, and saps my good health. I will no longer seek momentary pleasure in my mouth for such long range damage to my body. From now on that momentary pleasure will be recognized for the illusion that it really is. The taste of chocolate will be as bad as its effects. The taste of chocolate will no longer exist. Chocolate will instead taste like burnt rubber—bitter, acrid and uneatable.

Repetition of the last sentence, which is in every sense the punch line, will make this monologue increasingly effective. You can utilize the same idea for other fattening foods that do not automatically disappear from your natural eating habits, despite their absence from your "go" list. Pattern your monologue after this one, expressing your true thoughts about the dangers of the fattening food in question. Remember, your own belief in what you are saying to *yourself* is a fundamental prerequisite for success. You can use gimmicks, and tricks of the imagination to reinforce suggestion effects, but the basic suggestion—in this case, to eliminate a dangerously carbohydrate-packed food from your habits—must be thoroughly founded and believed.

More imaginative techniques

The Madison Avenue advertising men are constantly feeding *you* associative suggestions to enhance your liking for their product: "The new nylon that satisfies your craving for color." "Buy now. Why be left out in the cold." "Fried shrimps with that nut-like flavor." "The outlook is rosier, the feeling is cosier" (ad for a negligee).

To combat this, it may be necessary for you to use the same idea associations in reverse. Besides using taste associations, we can use other sensory or emotional tie-ins. "Why be left out in the cold" uses a sensory association that has been used so often it already packs an emotional punch. Eating ice cream can leave you out in the cold with the opposite sex. It can put ugly fat on you and make you unattractive.

"The outlook is rosier" suggests we might make gloom and doom a deterrent to some carbohydrate dandy. The rosy ad is pink with promise. Our gloom picture should be dark and dismal, fraught with danger, heavy with despair. It is a picture that goes well with heavy pies, thick gravies, and threatening cakes. Be your own Madison Avenue man. Paint your own mental picture. Instead of a come-on make it a strong come off-it.

You can also use your pet peeves to tack onto some of your persistent putters-on of weight. No love for policemen? Let the policeman force feed you. Have you an aversion to going to the dentist? Imagine your dentist having to drill and fill a cavity after every mouthful of sweets.

Your doctor-image, too, can come to your help in these associative suggestions. The most well-known act of the family doctor is to take out that little stick, and depress your tongue with it while you say "ahhh." More often than not you gag. If you gagged as readily on fatty carbohydrates, you would have no weight problem. Why not imagine yourself gagging on "stop" foods, the same way that you gag on the doctor's tongue-depressant?

It works. You feel repulsed by that food. The only trouble is that it sometimes works too well. You may find that you actually gag the next time that a "stop" food is on the way to your mouth. There is no need to carry things to this extreme in normal cases. If you do need a strong suggestion, and you try one such as this, drop it if it actually makes you gag or becomes a cause of unhappiness or discomfort.

How to cancel out a suggestion

If you have made a suggestion to yourself while in a state of deep relaxation, and its effects are not desirable or no longer wanted by you, it is very simple to wipe the slate clean.

For instance, in the case of the gagging just mentioned, you merely state that the "stop" food in question will no longer act as a tongue-depressant and cause gagging. Repeat this several times. You may have visualized yourself gagging on the food. If so, you will have to visualize yourself eating the food and not gagging. But be sure to put back a deterrent suggestion such as it tasting like fat as it drips down your throat to become fat on your body. Otherwise you will be faced with the persistance of your craving for the food in question.

Ending habitual hunger pangs

Your subconscious can strike back. If it has not caused you to misplace this book by this time, it may use its hungerpain producing power to get you back into the set eating ways to which it has become accustomed.

When you feel these pangs of hunger and you know you have eaten your fill of nourishing "go" foods less than a meal-time away, recognize these pangs for the trickery they are. You need not use willpower to ignore them. There are a number of simple ways to talk *yourself* out of them.

Sit down to a special relaxation period. Bring on the heaviness that produces deep relaxation. When you have attained a deep trance-like state of bliss, take your right hand off the arm of your chair (your left hand if you are a lefty) and place it in an imaginary bowl of warm water. The water is the same temperature as your hand. Or imagine hot water being added gradually so that the warmth is increased. The water is now just as hot as you like a bath to be. Now transfer your hand to your stomach. The warmth gives you a nice feeling. It is a comfortable, therapeutic feeling. It is a feeling of satisfaction, just as if you had eaten an adequate meal. Resolve that you will do this the next time that you feel a false or improper hunger. You will put your warm hand on your stomach and the hunger will disappear.

You will find this a quick and effective way to put off snack time or meal time. One deep session using this hand technique, will permit you to combat false hunger and those habit urges to eat when you need no food by the simple expedient of placing your hand on your stomach.

If this post-hypnotic suggestion begins to wear off before the poundage wears off, hold another special session and refill the imaginary bowl with hot water again. It will keep you out of hot water as you enjoy the thrill of seeing your weight progress chart dip lower and lower toward your promised land.

REVIEW

Reread the monologue on pages 133-134. Practice it in shortened form as outlined on pages 134-135. Then lengthen it in your own words and images to last one or two minutes of the total six minute procedure. Set a day and a time each week when you will conduct this six minute procedure. If your chart shows progress to be sluggish, step up the sessions to as often as once a day if necessary. Add more "disgusting" suggestions to attack carbohydrates that hang on. Cancel these suggestions if they prove bothersome.

11

HOW TO MAINTAIN AND CONTROL WEIGHT LOSS

Your period of weight loss has begun. You are on your way to being thin. This chapter will tell you how to control your weight loss, what you can expect to lose, and how long it will take to lose it. It will tell you what to do if your progress chart starts to dip too fast, or if at times *it* flattens out instead of you.

People react differently to what they eat or do not eat. Some lose fast, others slowly. Some may experience peaks and valleys in their progress charts as the process halts, even reverses temporarily; or as the progress accelerates suddenly for a brief spell. Only one thing is sure: everybody who is overweight will lose weight when off "stop" and "caution" foods and on "go" foods.

Setting your weight loss quota

You were instructed in Chapter 3 to draw a dotted line from your present weight down to what you feel is your right weight. You were told to allow 1% weight loss per week. The percentage of loss needed to attain your right weight is therefore that number of weeks in the future over which your dotted goal line should be plotted. If you wish to lose 30 pounds and you now weigh 150, this is a 20% loss. It should take about 20 weeks.

This 1% per week should be considered a maximum. It would not be safe for you to even expect to lose more than this. The word *expect* is used advisedly. Your expectations, now harnessed to the power of your subconscious, are going to count more than ever before.

The dotted quota line that you draw will be visualized in the weeks ahead when your suggestions are turned to imagining yourself thin. Part of the time that image will be your progress chart. You will see yourself the slender, erect person you really are, but you will also see the heavy line of your progress chart following the dotted quota line down gradually to your desired weight.

For those who wish to attain maximum speed of weight loss, a crash program, involving no more will power than expression of the wish, is set forth in the next chapter. It is advisable to set your goal at a little less than 1% right now. Later, if you do not attain this rate of loss, Chapter 13 will send the pounds spinning. Meanwhile, give yourself an extra few weeks than the 1% rule yields. There's no need to rush. You are gaining years of life expectancy. Draw the quota line on your chart right now, if you have not already done so.

A case of opposing powers

A librarian, 41, married but with no children had been suffering from overweight since childhood. At one point in her life she hit 200 lbs., then became quite ill. She was put on a diet of skimmed milk and bananas and lost 30 pounds in three months. But then she put the weight back on. She went to a new doctor. The pills he prescribed made her irritable and tense. She suffered from palpitations, chronic thirst, and insomnia. On October 31, weighing 171, she decided to turn to hypnosis. However, her decision vacillated in a way characteristic of her nervous condition. As a result, it took her a week to actually stop taking the pills and to make the firm agreement with herself to proceed wholeheartedly with the hypnotic suggestions. Naturally, her progress chart reflected this faltering start. On November 7 she still weighed 171.

During the second week she really settled down. She was now completely off the pills. The periods of relaxation combined with suggestions for serenity worked wonders for her. On November 14 she weighed 165. Two weeks later she weighed 159.

Then she became obsessed with the idea that all the weight she was now losing would return and that history would repeat itself. Her fears of regaining weight interfered with the effective process of suggestion and auto-suggestion. Her weight remained stationary for one week.

Again suggestion was used to restore confidence in her ability to accept her new eating habits as a permanent way of life. She was on no diet that she could get off, as before. With understanding, reinforced by suggestion, her fears were quieted and her progress chart resumed its downward slide. On December 27 she weighed 149. On January 8 she weighed 146½, the least she had ever weighed since girlhood. At last reports, she had stabilized her weight in the 130's, was no longer even thinking about it, and had become involved in organizing a county library system.

If you were to take a couple of minutes to chart this lady's weight changes, you would see several slopes instead of a steady downward progress. Each change in direction had to be coped with. The original hesitancy in her conviction, marked by a flat line at the beginning of the chart, had to be replaced with unshakable confidence. Later, when fear took over, her progress chart again leveled off and did not resume its downward movement until that fear had been removed.

You would be a rare person indeed if events in your life in the months ahead did not touch you emotionally in some way. Remember the school principal discussed in a previous

chapter? Her progress chart turned back upward for a few
days when school reopened. Similarly a family squabble can
stir up emotional forces that can temporarily eclipse your
newly acquired eating habits. Sudden business problems can
have the same effect.

Why you always win

What do we do then? Of course the solution in each case
will be tailor-made to fit the problem. However, every solution will have two important phases:

1. Facing up to the negativity of the incident and changing
   its polarity to positive.
2. Accelerating and lengthening your periods of relaxation
   and auto-suggestion.

These two phases are always a successful team. Whatever
the powers that oppose your weight loss, the power you exert
in these two steps is superior. The reason is simple: the first
step disarms the disrupting force; the second step reinforces
your own armament.

The first step in changing negative forces to positive ones
appears to be simple. Actually, it requires an amount of ob-
jectivity which the average person usually finds hard to muster
when involved in a worrisome or emotion-fraught situation.
You may realize that a headache is due to tension, but the
pain of it makes it even harder for you to relax. It helps to
have an aspirin available. Similarly, when you are suddenly
caught in a mesh of personality clashes, it is difficult if not
impossible to instantaneously and voluntarily turn hatred
into tolerance, resentment into understanding, or envy into
admiration.

A dramatic case in point concerns Diana Spencer Churchill,
daughter of Sir Winston Churchill, who had an unusual
voluntary job. She talked people out of suicide. Using her
middle name, Mrs. Spencer answered the phone, Mansion

House 900, maintained by St. Stephen's Church in London for people who were lonely or distressed and on the verge of suicide. Her duty was to listen to their tales of woe and then to change their emotional polarity with an inspiring, optimism-producing heart-to-heart talk. She saved many lives. But she could not do this for herself. She took her own life in 1963.

How can you cope with the every day emotional clouds that pass across your mental skies without outside help? Is there an emotional "aspirin" that you can administer to yourself to ease the tensions long enough to regain perspective and turn negative attitudes into positive ones? If you cannot do this, you are in for periods of regression in your weight loss as the disturbance gradually dominates your behavior.

There is a way for mature adults. It is simple, providing you have the awareness to remember it at a time when your attention is fairly fixed on your problem. Once remembered, you must also have the courage to give up your problem for a few moments to apply the technique. Although the way is easy, the awareness and the courage are not easy to come by. It is like asking the angry man to count to ten. It is perfectly obvious to everybody that counting to ten is a wise procedure at that moment—obvious that is, to everybody except the angry one.

Clip the wings of the crisis

If you are faced with an emotional crisis on the return of a chronic problem, here is what you can do. Go into your state of deep relaxation preparatory to auto-suggestion. Proceed with your auto-suggestions for weight control exactly as practiced. Then, prior to emerging, tell yourself that you would now like to understand more about the specific problem. Ask *yourself* these questions:

1. How can I prevent it from affecting my health?
2. What can I do to improve the situation?
3. How can I maintain a wholesome attitude about it?

After each question, pause and listen for the answer. It may come then, or it may take your limitless unconscious wisdom more time to deliver the right answer to you. You may wake up the next morning with the answer on your lips. Or the thought may strike you, as inspiration does, at any time.

After asking these questions and pausing for the answer, remind *yourself* of the following facts of life:

1. Sunshine always follows gloom, as day follows night.
2. The positive forces of creation are dominant over the negative forces of destruction.
3. Good always triumphs over evil.

Then as you are about to emerge, emphasize to *yourself* that you will awake "happy, optimistic and serene." Use this positive approach through auto-hypnosis freely. You need not be afraid of using it too often. Even when world affairs seem depressing to you, this technique will help you keep your own emotional keel level. President Kennedy's assassination affected many weight-reduction progress charts. It lessened the importance to people, subconsciously reduced their desire to lose. Giving depressed attitudes a positive "shot-in-the-arm" is a valuable use for self-hypnosis.

Evaluating your progress

Turning attention now to the normal progress of your weight loss, let us assume that no major crisis causes a sharp cessation or recession of your progress and let us examine instead the gradual slope of your progress chart in the first few weeks. What do we do when progress slows up? Can weight be lost too fast?

The 1% of your-weight-per-week rule has set your goal. But many factors will influence how close to that goal you actually come. You are not concerned with day-to-day fluctuations. In fact, one week may be too short a period in which to make a true evaluation. A change during a one week period should alert you to possible need for action.

An unmarried woman, age 38, and employed as a bookkeeper started her hypnosis treatment on November 26, weighing 179½. On December 1 she weighed 176, indicating an immediate response. On December 6 she weighed 175¼. This indicated that progress had stopped during the second five-day period. After a discussion, it was decided that there was no apparent outward cause for the slow-up, so no corrective action would be taken. In the next five days her weight dropped to 173 and she continued to lose one to two pounds per week in the weeks that followed.

Pauses like this in weight loss are common but often unexplainable. The tendency of the body to hold water can be affected by the amount of spice in food, or the amount of salt used. Two glasses of water can mean a pound. The process of ovulation can mean for women the build-up of several pounds of water prior to the menstrual cycle. Depriving yourself of drinking water may not affect water content in the body, as so many foods have an extremely high water content.

Other pauses in weight loss can only be surmised to have their causes in other changes in body chemistry or metabolism where a time element or time lag is involved. You can often sense a heavy or bloated feeling and not be able to attribute it to any particularly large meal. Other times your ring will feel tight, or your belt will feel more comfortable a notch looser than usual. These are indicative of times when the body weight is on the top side of its normally fluctuating cycle.

Getting your second breath

There will come a time when your progress pauses and you will have to do something about it. In fact, that pause may come in the first few weeks. If a man cuts down from 200 to 190 in the first month, he may note with gratification that he has followed his goal line down 1% a week precisely. Then he may find his progress halt for one, two, three weeks. If his weight loss does not then resume its downward trip, he must tighten up on his intake through reduced quantity suggestions during self-hypnosis. *I will be thoroughly satisfied with less quantity of "go" foods than I have been eating up until now.*

The body will often respond more quickly in the first few weeks of changed eating habits. There is a "soft" poundage in certain areas that is quick to go. Then the "hard" poundage is burned off at a slower rate. Also, an intake of food that causes a person to lose weight at 200 pounds, may be too much food to lose weight at 180 pounds. This means that you must go back into action during this period of "second wind" and step up your auto-suggestions.

If you are practicing relaxation and auto-suggestion once a week, increase the frequency to two or three times per week. Also, add the suggestion mentioned above, that you will be thoroughly satisfied on less quantity.

You will find that your appetite will be more easily satisfied. You may eat less often. There may even be one item of food that should have been blackballed but which has, through misunderstanding or a tricky, mutinous subconscious, been permitted to retain its place in your new eating habits. If it does not disappear with stepped up auto-suggestion, single it out for some of that special treatment outlined in the last chapter. You can also expel some foods from your "caution" list, if you are not losing weight. Do this through auto-suggestion. Tell *yourself* that this particular food is no longer on the "caution" list and has been placed on the "stop" list where it will no longer interest you.

Another step you can take is to check your own concept of certain foods. Study the recipe or container. Does it contain any sugar or starch. For instance, is the orange juice unsugared?

This is all you will need to do to get your "second wind"

and resume your weight loss. It may not be at a rate fast enough to match your enthusiasm, but remember: every pound lost is lost forever. A special "crash" program for rapid weight loss required under special circumstances is outlined in the next chapter.

How to stop losing

You have learned how to get the weight rolling off. Now, how do you stop it? Or, if you are losing too fast, how do you put the brakes on?

There are many factors that can suddenly cause your progress chart to dip sharper than the slope of your goal line. As your health improves, your metabolism may change. Pressure of business can also affect your metabolism rate. When the metabolism rate increases, fat is burned off faster. If you suspect a change in metabolism rate, you can check it out with your physician.

A change in jobs can affect your rate of weight loss. When Joe Louis retired from the ring and its rigorous road work, he gained weight. Contrarily, a secretary who became a dancing teacher, found that she had to eat more to keep her attractive curves.

If you are losing too fast, or if you have lost all you wish to lose, you can eat more and go more liberally into "caution" foods. Do either or both gradually. You do not need to condition yourself to do this. You merely halt your auto-suggestion sessions, then decide which caution foods to return to your menus.

The decision to add these foods is all that is necessary to find them tempting and appetizing to you again. This may seem surprising to you. It would seem to indicate that you can toss all your conditioning down the drain in one weak moment. But this is not so. You could not have such a weak moment while your weight loss was not what you have decided it should be. It is only the fact that your weight loss is progressing faster than you want, or has totaled all you want, that the mere decision to eat peas or peanuts is effective.

In effect, your subconscious has grasped the whole picture of the slimming process and will not resist any small changes that conform to the over-all goals, whether reached or being reached. So, all you do is decide to increase your intake of certain non-carbohydrate foods and the decision becomes a fact. Also any minor changes you make in your concept of "go" foods will become a fact.

You may find it a lot more difficult to return to your former fattening-up days. Remember when it was open house on sugar, sweets and starches? First, you will find it revolting even to think about. In the second place, you will find the decision unthinkable in the first place. So your eating habits are firmly established in a sensible, enjoyable way. You are relieved of the effort of exerting your will, ever again. Tips on how to more fully enjoy this new eating way of life will be given in Chapter 14. But first, Chapter 13 will outline a crash program for rapid weight loss for those who have decided to take as little time as possible for this important transition.

REVIEW

Perfect your progress chart. Mount it. Prepare sheets for the weeks ahead. Step up auto-suggestions to step up weight loss. Counteract the negative effect of crises with positive suggestions that brim with optimism.

12

PLANNING A WEIGHT LOSING CRASH PROGRAM

A 180-pound woman sat in the waiting room of the Nassau Institute for Hypnosis. Opposite her sat a chic, slim model whose clothes accented her 37-24-36 measurements. The heavier woman struck up a conversation with the attractive brunette on the wonders of hypnosis. She assumed that there was some problem such as smoking that was prompting the latter's visit. "No, I'm here to lose weight. I weigh 123 pounds and I must get back down to 116 fast or risk losing several of my accounts," explained the model.

Measuring up to the physical requirements of a job makes the process of losing weight big business in world centers of fashion and entertainment. Here the monumental incentive of keeping a job outweighs the other valid incentives that move most people to lose weight. Obviously it is a different problem for people who have never really been overweight to lose poundage than it is for a stout person. There are no vastly wrong eating habits to correct in most cases, unless there is a question of malnutrition involved. The problem becomes instead one of obtaining the maximum nutrition on the least amount of calories, and keeping to high protein foods to stimulate metabolism.

This chapter will provide you with an austerity program

for critical weight loss. It can be used by overweight persons who seek a crash program for rapid weight loss. It can be used by persons whose progress charts hit a snag and who need a good auto-hypnotic shove to send it tumbling again. And it can be used by slender persons who need to lose that difficult five or ten pounds required by their careers.

Important Note: You must follow all of the instructions leading up to this chapter. Instructions contained in this chapter only tell you how to shift into high gear once your weight loss has been started by the methods outlined on the previous pages.

One warning is in order for all who use this stepped-up program: It is equivalent to a rigid 600 to 1000 calorie diet and requires regular check-ups by a physician. Because you will need no will power, the danger of staying on this rugged regime too long is all the more real. It will probably cause the stout person to lose at a rate faster than the recommended maximum 1% per week. Depending on circumstances, weight can plunge as much as five pounds a week for a 200-pound person or 2½%. There is an additional danger, especially for lighter persons, of risking under-nourishment of the body if continued for more than a few weeks. Your physician can insure its proper application in your particular case.

How it works

If you were to prescribe the low-carbohydrate "go" food list as a "diet" to an interested overweight friend, you would probably be greeted with an indignant snort. "What! Give up ice cream? Cake? Spaghetti? Bread? Potatoes? Pie? What's so easy or miraculous about that? Sure, who wouldn't lose weight. But who wants to do it!" Yet your reaction was not like this. Once you understood how you had been brainwashed onto the carbohydrate kick, you were ready to cleanse the subconscious of its harmful conditioning; and recondition *yourself* with healthful habits.

If the crash program's daily food intake was now listed before you on this page, even though you are well along in your reconditioning program you would probably still throw up your hands in utter dismay. For the crash program not only shrinks the "go" list but places strict quantitative limits on everything.

You will see this list of daily food intake very soon in this chapter. However, before you set eyes on it, you would do well to remind yourself that you have a friend inside who will pull some strings to help you. Your subconscious will turn off the desire valve as soon as you have reached your special program limit. You will not need to exert that superhuman effort or suffer through the deprivation conjured up by the sight of the reduced intake.

After a brief talk with *yourself,* explaining the need for a temporary tightening up of food intake and providing *yourself* with appropriate post-hypnotic suggestions, what looks like a single lettuce leaf to you now will look like a brimming salad bowl later. What appears as a boring lack of choice to you now will appear to be a pleasantly diversified menu later.

One of the reasons that a physician's supervision is recommended is the utter ease with which you will embark on this program. The skill of relaxation and auto-hypnosis that you have already acquired will now provide you with the technique that will launch you effortlessly into a way of life where food becomes relatively unimportant for a brief period of time. It will be so effortless that you may not be willing to end that period when you really should. You may need a physician to remind you that your body is now losing weight too rapidly or that you have reached as low a weight as is healthful for you.

Changes in your "caution" list

The whole idea of a "caution" list changes in this crash program. And since it is the concept of the list rather than the items on it that becomes essential in the auto-conditioning process, let us first examine the new concept.

The business at hand is to lose excess weight fast and this crash program means business. The "caution" list you see here has been screened for carbohydrates with a fine-tooth comb. There are just enough carbohydrates in the foods on this list and on the new "go" list to provide your body with the fuel it needs for a normally active day. Higher activity than normal will induce an even more rapid weight loss and merit an even closer watch by your physician.

Read your new "caution" list. Visualize the foods on it, item by item. For the next few weeks these foods will be intermittently before you. They will provide you with vital nourishment, but must be eaten with the knowledge that they now become comparatively rich in carbohydrate for your new intake level. Eat them sparingly; make every mouthful go a long way. The foods on the "caution" list will not be mentioned by name here out of deference to those who wish to avoid them altogether. Examine the list if you wish to. Skip over it with your eyes if, instead, you wish to go the limit by restricting yourself to "go" foods on this crash program.

Changes in your "go" list

If you examine your "go" list you will recognize most of your favorites listed previously for your regular program of weight loss. All of the high protein meats are there—beef, pork, lamb, poultry. Some of the specialties like corned beef hash, canned luncheon meat and sausage have been removed because of their high fat content.

All the fish remain on the list, but frying as a method of preparation is now out. Poached, broiled, steamed, baked, even raw, but not fried in oil or fat.

Fats and oils remain on the list for a minimum of preparation processes and as salad dressing. Fruits and vegetables show very few changes.

CRASH LIST

	GO	CAUTION	STOP
Meat	Lean	Fatty	—
Fish	Lean	Fatty	—
Soup	Bouillon Consomme	Vegetable Onion	Others
Fruit	Grapefruit Melon Lemon	Strawberries Oranges Tangerines	Others
Juice	Tomato Vegetable Sauerkraut	Fresh orange Fresh grapefruit	Others
Vegetables	Asparagus Bamboo shoots Broccoli Cabbage Cauliflower Celery Chard Cucumbers Endive Lettuce Spinach Radishes Romaine Squash (summer) Sprouts Tomatoes Water cress	Chives Eggplant Leeks Okra Pumpkins Squash (winter) Turnips Artichokes Beets Brussel sprouts Carrots Onions	Others
Eggs	Prepared without fat	—	—
Cheese	Cottage cheese (regular or skimmed)	Others	—

Beverages	Tea	Low calorie	Others
	Coffee	sodas (1 glass	
	Lemonade (lemon juice,	daily)	
	artificial sweetener)		
	Skimmed milk		

STOP—MISCELLANEOUS

Bread	Nuts	Jams
Rolls	Pies	Preserves
Cakes	Puddings	Gravies
Cookies	Salad dressings	Beer
Crackers	Sandwiches	Wines
Cereals	Sauces	Liqueurs
Fats	Sweets	Sodas
Flour	Macaroni	Sugar
Ices	Spaghetti	Sorbitol (sweet-
Ice Cream	Jellies	ening agent)

The biggest change in the "go" list concept is in terms of quantity. The idea of unlimited intake of steak, salmon or scrambled eggs must now give way to the idea of paucity, frugality and conservation. Before, it was—eat all you want. Now it still is—eat all you want—but you *want* to eat *less* and lose more. Self-hypnosis will help you to do this effortlessly, but right now you must understand the new meaning of your "go" list. Go, but go with prudence.

The temporary aspect of this program raises the question: Is this a diet? When I get off it will I start to regain just as I do getting off any type of diet? The answer is yes and no. By definition, yes, this is a diet. But no, you will not regain when you get off it, because you will go back to low-carbohydrate eating ways. You will stop losing, but there is very little likelihood of your gaining back any substantial amount of lost weight. Should anything in life's circumstances tend to make carbohydrates in the least tempting to you again, you now have the knowledge to be aware of what is happening and what to do about it. A few reinforcing auto-hypnotic sessions puts you back on the healthful track immediately.

Eat less and like it

When you used suggestions for your original "go" list, there was no restriction in the concept of the foods on that list. Eat all you want of these foods was the order of the day. However, your new "go" list carries with it a built-in idea: *limit yourself*. Extravagance must give way to frugality on the crash program. Preparation to use auto-suggestion on this new "go" list must therefore include a quantitative agreement with yourself, as well as qualitative.

To get across this idea of rationed allotment, such words as portion, serving, and ounce, must enter into our procedure. Food amounts must be defined. However, these definitions and numerical boundaries are not mandatory. They are recommended maximums. Rigidity has the characteristic of containing the seeds of its own destruction. Don't impose memorized cup, ounce, and portion limits on *yourself*. Instead, convey the idea of paucity with permissiveness. Don't say, here is 38 cents—spend just that. But rather, here is 50 cents —spend all you have to.

People who desire to lose weight fast for a brief period will find it just as effortless to shift into an "eliminate quantity" eating pattern as they originally did in shifting to an "eliminate carbohydrate—heavy foods" regime. Your subconscious, properly instructed, will see to that.

The first step is to analyze the quantity aspect rationally, see how it shapes up, then agree to embark. With this agreement comes the confidence and belief necessary for successful auto-hypnosis. So let us take the plunge and see what a "normal" day on the crash program will be like.

In the morning you rise and dress. You plan your activities for the day. Somehow breakfast does not seem important, but a half of grapefruit would be nice. You enjoy its tangy zest

You cover up the other half in wrap or foil and put it back in the refrigerator. Perhaps you are cooking eggs for the family anyhow, how about one for yourself. What will it be this morning—poached, boiled, scrambled? Two cups of hot, black, coffee and you are on your way.

You suddenly realize it's way past noon you had better have some lunch. You make or order a crisp salad with tomatoes, cucumbers, radishes, celery leaves and chase it with a tall glass of skimmed milk. Later in the afternoon you have a cup of coffee or a pot of tea as a pick-me-up.

The indifferent attitude regarding breakfast and lunch has disappeared by dinner time. You enjoy planning and shopping for it. Lamb chops tonight. You tell the butcher to trim the fat. You select some fresh or frozen vegetable, fruits and needed staples. Dinner is a satisfying experience: two savory lamb chops, boiled just right; fancy asparagus; boiled tender white onions. Dessert is stewed rhubarb and coffee. Later that evening you raid the icebox and polish off the rest of that morning grapefruit, or you eat an orange.

How much more enjoyable it is to visualize the day's quantitative allotment this way. Here is how this would look in a typical rigidly regimented diet:

Breakfast: One grapefruit or one orange, one egg, coffee or tea.

Lunch: One or two servings of salad, one or two glasses of skimmed milk.

Dinner: One average portion of lean meat or fish, one or two servings of vegetables, ½ cantaloupe.

The kind of food we enjoy eating is a product of conditioning, and likewise the quantity we enjoy eating is a product of conditioning. There are records of fasting for months on end where the whole idea of eating departed from the thinking pattern of the person after the first few days. The body does not miss food to the extent that our conditioned reflexes would have us believe. In fact, temporary periods of fasting have more often than not acted as a boon to the health level of the body, apparently by giving the body a rest from the complicated, continuous tasks of digestion and excretion.

Your body will welcome this temporary respite from the labors of full-steam-ahead digestion. It has stored up many of the essential nutrients it needs. There is a sufficiency of the unstored nutrients in your new regimen. If your physician believes you need to be bolstered with concentrates in any department, he will prescribe them.

Water is not included in the concept of frugality. Nature's solvent may be imbibed at will. It will cleanse and purify your body. It will not add to your weight over the duration of your crash program.

Later in this chapter you will be given ideas and recipes for adding gourmet touches and interest to your "go" foods. But first, you have a job to do. You must review in your own mind the new concept of your "go" list. You must be willing to adopt it wholeheartedly as your way of life for a number of weeks ahead.

As soon as you make the decision, proceed to the next step: instructing your subconscious of your intent.

New instructions to your subconscious

You are now ready to use the miraculous powers of autosuggestion you have learned and have presumably already applied for a period of time. All that changes is the list you hold in your hand and the specific suggestion you give to *yourself*. Once *you* receive those suggestions, *you* will respond by behaving exactly as you visualize without hunger pangs or adjustment pains.

Reviewing the procedure, the basic steps are as follows:

1. You sit comfortably in a straight back chair, preferably with arms. A table with your "go" list on it is at hand.

2. You relax deeply and blissfully, using your preferred technique to carry you swiftly into a trance-like hypnotic state.
3. You give yourself the proper suggestions, picking up your "go" list at the appropriate time.
4. You emerge alert and refreshed.

Since it is only step 3 that changes, here is the substance of the crash program suggestions to give yourself. They are outlined below in similar fashion to the regular program monologue suggestions outlined on pages 134-135 in Chapter 10. These are the pertinent thoughts and images that go into your new "go" list monologue:

1. I am relaxed and breathing deeply.
2. I am aware of my body, toes to head.
3. I look into the future and see myself thin.
4. I pick up my "go" list of foods.
5. I will be perfectly satisfied with these foods.
6. I visualize myself eating frugally.
7. I find it unnecessary to eat any "stop" foods.
8. I am not particularly interested in "caution" foods.
9. I see myself becoming slender, faster, without hunger.
10. My next session will be quicker and deeper.
11. I emerge alert and refreshed.

You will note that, aside from a few slight changes in the thoughts, only one new suggestion in the sequence of suggestions has been added: number 6. This is, of course, the suggestion having to do with the control of quantity, the key to your crash program. Imagining yourself eating frugally is that key. How well you do this will determine your success. Picture that half a grapefruit, the one egg. See yourself wrapping the other half of grapefruit and putting it back in the refrigerator. Feel the enjoyment of eating the one egg and washing it down with fresh, hot black coffee.

Can you see the salad bowl? What vegetables are in it? It's crisp, delicious, and filling. You have a tall glass of skimmed

milk and can hardly finish it all. You are full. You see yourself at the dinner table. Your dinner plate is full. It has on it
a thick slice of juicy roast beef, some broiled mushrooms and
a serving of french-style string beans. You see yourself eat
leisurely, chewing slowly and savoring every mouthful. You
think, "My, what a big meal this really is."

The essence of quantity limitation is to experience visually,
in self-hypnosis, the actual quantity to which you limit yourself, picturing yourself entirely satisfied with that quantity.
Note that to explain this adequately, actual foods and portions were used which had previously been used in the typical
day's intake specified a few pages earlier. The grapefruit was
cut in half, the other half wrapped and put back in the refrigerator. This brings the quantity limit into better focus. You
are better able to image in hypnosis if you have previously
reviewed these limits consciously and rationally at some previous time.

In fact, it would be far better for you yourself to work out
a series of daily menus, including the size of the portions, than
it would be for these to be specified for you. By working them
out yourself, you concentrate on the actual spoon you will use
to serve the string beans. You decide how many make a moderate serving. Later in auto-suggestion, when you visualize
yourself enjoying a moderate portion of string beans *you* know
just what you are talking about.

How to establish typical menus

The suggested day's menu on page 166 can be the guide in
preparing a week or two of menus, each day different from
the rest. The one thing that they will have in common is the
exact image in your mind of how much a portion or a serving is.

The more exact that image is, the more unswerving will be
your full satisfaction with the portion you give yourself. An
undefined portion, blurred in your own mind, will yield ques-
tionable satisfaction at the close of the meal. A sharply focused

portion, understood and consented to, will yield complete satisfaction at the close of the meal.

The reason for this is simple. Your subconscious will obey your visualized instructions. If you do not visualize a clear cut portion satisfying you, there is no point at which the subconscious can signal "enough!" If your camera is out of focus, the picture it delivers cannot be sharp.

The definitions *you* make for yourself need not be the exact number of string beans, or the circumference of the grapefruit. Visualize that part of the dinner plate that a serving normally occupies, or if you eat at home and use a particular utensil, visualize yourself going through the motions of placing a moderate serving on the dinner plate. There are grapefruits that are selected for size and sold by the pound. These monstrous specimens, twice the normal fruit, are, of course, not what you visualize slicing down the middle. It is the average grapefruit that you are accustomed to using which belongs in that image. If you are accustomed to using the big specimens, hats off to you; you know a good thing and have earned your reward!

In preparing a series of menus, work from your total day's allotment and divide the quantities any way you wish. Try to retain the same over-all importance for each meal, as this will help to condition you. Here are the foods and quantities thereof prescribed for one day:

One grapefruit, ½ melon, and one orange.
One egg, and one average portion of lean meat or fish.
Two servings of "go" vegetables.
Two servings of salad.
Two glasses of skimmed milk.
Coffee or tea at will.

If you are confronted with a "caution" food and it is socially expedient for you to indulge, a good formula to follow is: one serving of caution food equals two servings of a "go" food.

Here are two more days as they might be set up:

	Day #2	Day #3
Breakfast:	Tomato juice Two slices Canadian bacon Coffee	½ cantaloupe 1 poached egg Coffee
Lunch:	Cup of clear boullion Cottage cheese ½ grapefriut Tea or coffee	Mixed green salad Jello Glass of skimmed milk

Dinner:	Celery, radish,
	  carrot sticks
	Broiled fish
	Spinach
	Melon
	Tea or coffee
		Cup of consomme
		Broiled hamburger
		  steak
		Cauliflower
		½ grapefruit
		Tea or coffee

You will note that an item has been added here or there, but another is then removed. The exchange is equal if they are "go" items, one for two if the substitute comes from the "caution" list.

It is essential that you build your own menus rather than memorize these. They are provided only as a guide. Try your hand at a few prior to your first "crash program" auto-hypnosis session. You will find it a simple matter, then, to visualize step 6 and to etch into your subconscious through imagining the quantity limitations. Do this now. Then conduct your first "crash program" relaxation and suggestion session outlined on pages 163-165.

How to end the crash program

Hopefully, you will accomplish your "crash program" purpose in a few weeks. Do not continue it more than five weeks without the permission of your family physician. Put a vertical line on your progress chart on the date you start the "crash program." Measure five weeks ahead and put another vertical line as a reminder of the deadline when terminating it.

When you reach your desired weight loss, or the deadline date, whichever happens first, all you need do to go back to your original "go" list is to conduct one auto-hypnotic session with your original "go" list, in the same manner as you originally conducted it. This session will cancel the strict limitations set up by the "crash program." It will return your conditioning to eating all you want of the "go" foods. Review these "go" foods in your own mind once more and take another look at the "caution" foods as originally prepared in Chapter 9.

As your progress chart shows a descending line, your scale a lower reading, and your mirror a new you, your weeks or months of auto-conditioning will have paid off. You will have become accustomed to a new, higher level of life's enjoyment and others will be enjoying you. You can review all the material now until this time arrives. Then, when your progress chart shows the glorious goal reached, you can resume reading Chapter 14 on how to stay thin; how to get the most out of your new philosophy about food; and how to resist any unwanted suggestions from the world about us and its continuing "carbohydrate barrage."

REVIEW

Rewrite your caution list. Change your "go" list, too, visualizing the foods on it just the way you like them. Then recondition yourself to these new lists through several self-hypnosis sessions, introducing quantity-limiting suggestions. Be sure to picture the actual size of portions to which you are limiting yourself. Check weight regularly. End "crash" program as soon as weight loss reaches desired level; do not continue it longer than five weeks. (The period of crash diet is between you and your physician.)

13

HOW TO STAY THIN
AND ENJOY DOING IT

One day the line on your progress chart will reach the goal you have set for your desired weight. It will be an occasion for celebration. However, chances are the festivities that ensue will not include an iced cake with a candle for every pound, nor will you be surrounded by beer and pretzels. You may find, instead, that you will invite your friends to a clambake or a luau. Or treat the family to a beefsteak party. You may even decide on a drive in the country instead. Your habits—even for celebrating—have changed, and it will take more than the final square in your progress chart to change them back again.

Actually, your celebration will probably have already started long before you reach your goal. You will have begun to feel an exuberance hard to contain. Your spirits and your energy will have soared and your enthusiasm and zest for life will have made every day and night seem festive compared to the obese days of months gone by.

Will this ever change? Are there forces that will work to restore the carbohydrate foods to your daily eating pattern? If so, will it happen gradually or all of a sudden, and how can these forces be combatted? The answer is yes, there are such forces; forces that will gradually recondition you if you let them, and forces that will try to transform you quickly if you let them. This chapter will help you recognize these forces and tell you the simple counter-measures that you can take to vanquish any of life's influences toward a return to sweets and starches. Here, then, is how to *keep* yourself thin.

Here comes that bombardment again

The carbohydrate bombardment via the television circuits and the air waves is still on. It never stopped. It smiles at you from billboards, greets you from pastry-filled lunch counters, and cultivates you at every social opportunity. Are you now permanently invulnerable to its effects? Decidedly not. Were you to think you were immune and not strengthen your re-sistance, there would bound to come a time when your eating habits would once more resemble those of Mr. and Mrs. Fat-ten Easily.

You are now invulnerable. But you must reinforce your auto-conditioning from time to time if you are to stay invul-nerable. All this takes is a quiet conversation with yourself once in a while. That same room, that same chair, that same quick descent into a state of blissful quiet, that same picturing of the disgusting drip of fat down your throat which eating carbohydrates means, that same "go" list, and the quick ex-uberant return to full wakefulness—and continued invulner-ability. Is this worth ten minutes once a month, or even once every two months? It should be.

The effect of this is to neutralize the voices that shout at you daily to eat sweets and get that quick lift, or to buy cake mix and be the admired kitchen expert. These voices now ring hollow. You recognize them for what they are. But they are heard, they do get recorded in the vast subconscious, they do build up a cumulative effect. One day, if permitted to build up a large enough potential, they may be strong enough to motivate you gradually in the direction they want, and away from the direction you want.

So, even if you are squarely on the beam and now feel no sense of temptation from the fatty villains of yesterday, take those ten minutes off from your busy, happy, energetic day once in a while to recondition yourself and wash your subconscious clean of unwanted suggestions before those few loiterers form a crowd.

How to face the inevitable crisis

Environmental changes that can interrupt your weight loss and that were described in Chapter 11 can also act to change your weight up or down in your slender years ahead.

A housewife who reduced her weight from 190 to 135 in seven months of hypno-therapy came back a year later. She weighed 158. Her weight started to climb back on a Tuesday, six weeks before. That was the day she received a letter from her vacationing husband saying that he had taken somebody with him whom he loved and he was not coming back.

What should be done in this case? Obviously, reminding the subconscious about the fattening aspects of carbohydrates will not solve the problem. If anything, it might cause a serious conflict and only make the problem worse. In fact, in this woman's case she had lost her whole purpose for losing weight in the first place. She now had no husband to please.

Still, hypnotism helped her, administered both by the author and by herself. There was nothing she could do about the crisis. When other people are involved, we are often powerless to intervene and change their behavior. But their behavior does not make us any less of a person than we were before. This was the essence of the suggestion used: that she was still the capable, attractive person she always was and that she was still on the path of a rewarding and fruitful life. Intensive use of these suggestions in a visual manner restored her self-confidence and reinstated her previous program for proper eating.

Personality clashes

A crisis may not be as well defined as a postman's ring. It may not even be recognized when it arrives. It may come "on little cat's feet" of hostility, resentment or jealousy. One would be likely to refuse to admit that it was actually there.

A beautiful girl in her early twenties gained some weight shortly after her marriage. Her mother chided her for it. She, too, was a good-looking person and anxious that her daughter stay attractive. However, the admonitions to eat less began to have the opposite effect. It would send the daughter on an eating rampage. In effect, she was saying to her mother, "I'll lose when I want to."

Here was a case of hostility that was obvious and irrefutable when pointed out to the girl. There was no stopping the mother. What could the girl do for herself? Here is the monologue that she agreed to use in self-hypnosis sessions:

> *I am aware of the feelings I have toward my mother. By allowing my mind to dwell on her, my mind has made my mother instrumental in my being overweight. As I relax I become aware of the presence of my body. My legs, my thighs, my stomach, my chest, my shoulders, my neck, my arms. I begin to feel a sensitivity as if I can feel the dimensions of my body, its girth. When I lose this girth I will feel the slimness. As I lose weight, I will be the beneficiary. I will enjoy the health and attractiveness. I will lose weight for myself. I am calm and determined.*

There is one common denominator to all emotional crises which can be taken into account in dampening the effect on your good eating habits. That is, there is no valid connection between the crisis and the cream. Carbohydrates will not solve the problem. If anything, you are compounding the problem—with fat. There is no escape from the problem by hiding behind a napkin. You emerge with the problem still there and another one—obesity—to boot.

If you understand and agree, then here is a common denominator monologue which you can use in self-hypnosis sessions. It will help destroy or head off any effect that a particular crisis may have on your good eating habits:

> *I imagine myself sitting between two other selves. On my left I sit very heavy, very obese, uncomfortable with fat, awkward and unhealthy. I sit there on my left with the problem of* (state problem). *On my right I see my other self. This self is slender and vital, trim and vibrant. My thin self has this same problem. I can select to have this problem as the fat person on my left or as the slender person on my right. Of course, I select to be the person on my right. It is the only intelligent solution.*

Not all problems can be solved without help. "If pain persists, see your doctor" is a truism that applies here, too. In extreme cases, seek help. That help can assist you in facing up squarely to the problem and prevent your escaping in other directions. Also, you can use your self-hypnosis sessions to sit in a relaxed, receptive mood seeking the answer to your problem.

Mining for coal or ideas

Many people make drastic changes in their environment. They change from a working life to a non-working life. Or they change from a job requiring vast physical exertion to one behind a desk. Some men get promoted from line jobs requiring their being on their feet most of the day, to administrative jobs that use only that much energy needed to push a pencil, lift a telephone, or come up with an occasional good idea. Not that good ideas do not burn fuel. They do, and some men burn more fuel coping with desk problems than do coal miners. But, more often than not, the switch is significant. Some women acquire a maid and switch to canasta. Others may be forced to give up leisure time and take to the vacuum cleaner.

All of these changes should produce equivalent changes in our eating pattern. As less energy is required, we should feel satisfied with less food. But in most cases, the small voice of intuition is drowned out by the louder cry of habit. You eat the same. Therefore, you gain weight.

You will have to use those same suggestions regarding the limitation of quantity as you did in Chapters 12 and 13. Visualize the actual quantity of food you were eating before and the actual work you were doing. Visualize a thermometer with a high reading to denote the great energy you were consuming. Then visualize your new job. The thermometer has dropped. The quantity of food is lower, too. "I will be thoroughly satisfied with less quantity, because I know my body needs less."

Recognizing the two-pound danger signal

Because of the vigilance needed to combat forces that will try to make you fat again, it is advisable to keep a weekly check on your weight. In fact, many have found it useful to keep up their progress chart despite the boringly flat horizontal line that it becomes. It serves to alert you to any change and start you thinking about what to do about it.

One step further that can also be helpful to the continuation of your dotted goal line on the progress chart. This dotted line extends into the future along your present weight line. By drawing it ahead on your progress chart, you are helping to "blueprint" your future weight. You are giving your subconscious a powerful suggestion that will act continuously to help you for as long as the chart is kept up.

The line may not be absolutely flat. There will be minor fluctuations. One pound up or down should not be considered significant. However, should your weight show a two-pound rise that is maintained for several days, consider that the danger signal to go into self-hypnosis action.

If this two-pound rise came right after you had hit your goal and had discontinued your sessions, chances are you did not completely eliminate a desire or craving for a particular food. Your sessions should be continued once or twice a week and you should include some suggestions aimed at that trouble-making food, as described in Chapter 11.

If this two-pound rise comes later, this is a different matter. Something has happened to upset your habits. The non-smoker never "returns" to smoking. The teetotaler never "returns" to drink. Neither have a craving or even the slightest desire or they would have tended to satisfy that desire at some time. You are a teetotaler of rich and fattening foods. If you gain two pounds, something has happened to change that fact. Whatever it is that is hitting you, as described earlier in this chapter, you will have to hit back hard just the way you did when you began your self-hypnosis sessions. Except, now you will have a head start. You will be a skilled relaxer and, with just a brief review of one or two chapters, will know just how to give yourself suggestions that will be powerful antidotes to fattening poison, effective immediately.

How to enjoy your food

You have conquered your compulsion for fattening food. You are not on a diet. You are not acting the part of a proper eater. You *are* one. Compulsion has become subservient to intelligence. Without forcible control, you eat whatever you want knowing you want whatever you need.

There is no change in your "go" list, "caution" list, or "stop" list. You still go, you still stop, and you never throw caution to the winds. Your one control valve is this "caution" list. You can provide yourself with some leeway by exercising more caution or less caution. If you lose two pounds, you add peas and lima beans more liberally, as well as other fruits and vegetables on the list. If you gain two pounds you go easy for a while on "caution" foods.

You are no longer as constantly concerned about food as you used to be. There probably was a time not too long ago when you lived from pastry to pizza pie as stepping stones between meals. Now you eat to satisfy your need for nourishment and energy. This does not mean that your enjoyment of good food is lessened. In fact, where sugar and refined flour were once your gauges for what tasted good, enjoyment is now measured naturally by such more valid criteria as freshness, flavor, and perfection. In short you are a step closer to being a gourmet.

Eating is now an even more important occasion. The table is set with good taste and inviting decor. Meals are leisurely. You chew your food slowly and well, savoring the flavor and getting maximum enjoyment from each mouthful. You recall the day when you bolted your food down, eating hoggishly more in five minutes than you now eat in 15, and enjoying it less. You might just as well have had the food inserted directly into your stomach for all the true enjoyment you got out of it. Like promiscuous sex, it yields a quantity of indulgence but no lasting significance. Today, you and your food have a mutual understanding, and every meal is a fulfillment.

Your new lease on life

Many people who arrive at a long-sought goal have a letdown feeling on reaching it. Post-natal depression can plague mothers. Divorces often take place after a new home is built or after wealth is acquired. You are slender, happy, energetic, healthy and attractive. Now what?

There is a saying that anticipation is far greater than realization. Perhaps another way to word it is: habitual anticipation leaves a void when dissolved by realization. That void is what produces the depression.

The answer is to fill the void. Substitute new anticipation.

Life without challenge, without unreached goals is an empty life indeed, regardless of how full of material wealth it may appear to be. The mountain climber's answer to the question of why he must climb Mt. Everest is now classic: "Because it is there."

Even the little unborn chick must have its challenge. Help it break the egg and it soon dies. It is as if challenge is the essence of life. Without challenge, life can be meaningless; strength and resources bound into action. The person who sets goals and rises to challenges, is a person girded for living, reaching new plateaus of maturity, drawing security from Nature's abundance, abounding with inspiration and energy, and attuned to the very life force by which we grow.

REVIEW

Ten minutes once a month devoted to self-hypnosis will neutralize ten hours or more of carbohydrate bombardment. Watch for emotional peaks and valleys. Even them out with quantity suggestions and stimulating suggestions. If you change your job, you may have to alter your eating habits again through self-hypnosis.

14

REMEMBER— YOU'RE GIVING UP NOTHING BUT UGLY, FAT POUNDS

To be of any value all teaching must be in depth. To superficially gloss over any technique or knowledge will glean for you only an inkling of it, and that inkling may soon slip away from you. Whereas, to study, experience, explore, identify, associate, discriminate, practice and visualize will produce for you a new body of information and skill that is permanently yours.

To attain quick and dramatic results from the technique taught in this book, you must be willing to put the book down and practice relaxation and suggestion each progressive step of the way. It is hoped that by the time you have reached this last chapter you have already started on the first chapter of your new slim-without-effort life. By now your progress chart should be indicating the downward course your weight will be taking, as you retire this book to the shelves for occasional future reference.

On the other hand, if you have been absorbed in reading it through to the exclusion of practice, now is the time to begin to use the tools that each chapter provides, while memory is fresh and enthusiasm high.

Hypnotism has vast usage

Hypnotism, once the unfortunate handmaiden of mysticism, is now the recognized and valuable tool of physicians, dentists, psychiatrists, psychologists, obstetricians, gynecologists and others in the medical arts. What is more, all hypnotism is recognized to be self-hypnotism. What the hypnotist brings about in you, you can bring about in yourself.

Self-hypnotism is safe. You are never in danger any more than you are in danger when you are asleep. In fact you are more aware of the doorbell, other noises, smells, or any other events around you than if you were napping. The self-imposed state of hypnotism is a deep state of relaxation, short of sleep. In this state you can talk to *yourself* (the subconscious), visualizing suggestions and instructions that later become an automatic part of effortless behavior.

The use of self-hypnosis in conquering bad habits and improving desirable skills is essentially a standard procedure regardless of the habit or the skill. The first step of that procedure is to arrive at a decision and write it down. In the case of weight control, we decide to combat the carbohydrate "bombardment" and we write down the foods that will be part of our new balanced eating way. The second step is to go into deep relaxation. The final step is to make proper constructive suggestions to *yourself*. Visualize your suggestions wherever possible. Pictures in the mind are worth a thousand words.

These three steps—decision, relaxation, suggestion—can be used successfully to stop smoking or play a better game of golf. It can be used to mold personality and improve salesmanship. The success of hypnotism and self-hypnotism in all aspects of human behavior should serve to bolster your own confidence in its successful use by you to lose weight.

It also has vast power

Lest over-confidence lead to carelessness in its use, one last word is in order about the immense power of self-hypnosis. It should not be used frivolously, nor should you experiment with its use on seemingly innocent matters. Stick to the text basically in its application for permanent weight loss. Seek professional advice if you wish to use the method on other problems.

The great miracle of being able practically overnight to crave the right foods instead of the wrong foods by such simple self-taught devices may tempt you to teach self-hypnosis to others. This could be unwise, as you would be putting very powerful tools in the hands of persons who may not have the benefit then of the many safety measures that have been built into this text. Lend or recommend the book, but do not assume the responsibility of taking its place.

This should not make you feel that there is any risk in using the techniques taught here or in following the directions for weight loss, even rapid weight loss. As long as you observe the precautions that are also spelled out, the techniques can only benefit and help you. It is always preferable to have a psychologist, physician, hypnologist or other professional person assist you in self-hypnosis, but in the absence of such help, you can be led by the book safely and successfully along the gratifying road to lasting slimness.

Make your decision

The do-it-yourself project in hypnotism differs from sessions with a professional hypnotist. In the case of the latter, about all you have to do is remember to keep the appointments. The hypnotist does the rest. But like any do-it-yourself project, self-hypnotism requires that you be a self-starter.

You must remember to keep the appointment with yourself. Then you must apply yourself conscientiously to each step in the decision-making stage of establishing your "go" foods; in the relaxation stage that gets deeper, quicker each time you try; and in the suggestion stage that brings about the instantaneous habit transformations.

The decision to lose weight through self-hypnosis is an easier decision to make than to embark on a diet. You know it involves no giving up of wanted foods. It merely changes your wants. There are no false starts, no last fling, no "I'll start tomorrow."

Your will is put to no test by having to say "no" to some tasty dish. There is no temptation to eat some fattening food. Instead, your taste buds are retrained, reeducated. Knowing that this is what happens and that there is no sacrifice involved, the decision to adopt "go" foods and reject the "stop" foods is a perfunctory one, requiring no more resolve than that original decision to lose weight, look better and live longer which led you to this book.

Practice relaxation

It should be easy to remember your self-hypnotism appointments to relax. These periods are healthful, energizing, and restorative. You will look forward to the few minutes that you take out from your daily schedule to practice the deep relaxation that is the key to self-hypnosis.

You will find these periods of relaxation helpful in many ways. They will lessen the tensions that cause many of us to acquire wrong eating habits in the first place. You will get to know yourself better in these quiet moments. You will find out just what thoughts persist in occupying your conscious mind when you try to quiet it. You will meet the real you, not the cocktail party self that talks about the weather or the spouse concerned with family, but the true self that seeks expression and unfoldment, that yearns to terminate endless wanderings in the maze of life and to realize grand potentials.

Most important, your periods of deep relaxation will bare

your subconscious so that you can change the foods it motivates you to eat. As you quiet down, then escalate yourself into a deeper state of relaxation, you are opening the doors to your subconscious. Once open, your instructions to it then become implicity obeyed. Like a great vault, you can change the combination and set the time lock. Is your craving mechanism now set for french fried potatoes, chocolate layer cake? Presto, it is changed to savory string beans and tangy grapefruit.

Only through sincerely applying the techniques of relaxation can this come about. But once applied, the ability to relax is never lost, and every session is even more successful than the one before.

Visualize your suggestions

Pushing the buttons that reset your motivations is the easiest job of all. If you have found it easier to dream about being thin than becoming thin, then self-hypnotism is for you. For it is made of dreams, a kind of day-dreaming visualization with a purpose.

These images that are conjured up by the imagination are the shadows of things to come. When they are held by you while in a state of deep relaxation, things come sooner. In fact they can come immediately. For example, if you used the "obnoxious" techniques to hypnotize yourself out of a craving for candy—visualized a dentist drilling your tooth after your next bite—you would be a long time taking that next bite; so long a time that you would have lost the craving permanently and probably substituted something more healthful in its place.

However, most suggestions you will be giving yourself will be pleasant ones. You will enjoy picturing yourself thin in your smart new clothes, seeing yourself gaining a new acceptance among your friends and being more attractive to the opposite sex. You will enjoy picturing the lusty foods on your "go" list and visualizing the delicious ways you will prepare them.

All of these pleasant mental pictures, entertained while in an enjoyable state of deep relaxation, will in effect reset the motivating mechanism within you from position A, that has made you what you are today, to position B that now makes you what you want to be.

Why you don't need to diet

The main reason hypnotism is being used so successfully throughout the country by people with weight problems is that it does not force them to stay on a diet. Instead it makes them wake up the next morning automatically wanting to eat the right foods.

You do not have to have the courage today to resolve to give up fattening foods. You do not have to have the will power to follow through on any such resolve. You do not have to count calories, do without second portions, or forego coffee breaks and midnight snacks. All you have to do is use the instructions in this book to practice how to relax and how to use auto-suggestion.

Gone are the days of blaming yourself for not resisting temptation, the mortifying days of finding your weight back where you started from, the days regimented with planned menus, sweated and vibrated days. Gone are the days of sacrifice, sacrifice and still more sacrifice only to find that your will to sacrifice is now a frail, broken reed in the windstorm of habit.

Instead, as close as tomorrow, are days of renaissance. You will feel reborn as your whole personality responds to your own life-giving suggestions. A vital part of you will be renewed, a part of you that has been crying for renewal. This new slim, trim you will then face a new and rewarding life of fun and success.

That many of the forests on earth are bogged down by an

infestation of vines is a sad obstacle to their growth. That a tree is never quite able to reach the sunlight is a mishap in Nature's scheme of things. Man has conquered the elements and most of his natural enemies. He now has but to conquer himself. It might be called the last step up the ladder of evolution.

Man's capability is little understood and only partially tapped. Now we hear more frequently that man is using only a fraction of his mind's capacity. The seriousness with which man is now studying phenomena of the mind considered taboo a decade ago opens up new paths for his perfectibility. Turning the mind on itself, as we do in self-hypnosis, is a skill that can lead to higher and higher peaks of self-mastery. The loss of unwanted habits and the development of creative skills constitute a rocky road to that self-mastery. The skill that you have learned through this book—the ability to quickly attain a deep, blissful trance-like state of relaxation and to make constructive suggestions to *yourself*—can be valuable to you in both the loss of many bad habits and development of many good ones. With it you can cope with such problems as smoking, insomnia, excessive drinking, and migraine headaches. You can reach right into your subconcious and turn off speech defects, gum chewing or nail-biting and turn on salesmanship, memory power, or sexual vigor. It can be an effective catalyst to good health, a maturing philosophy, and peace of mind.

As you now begin in earnest your deep relaxations and powerful weight losing auto-suggestions, all is quiet. You have chosen a comfortable chair. It is dark and still. It is the moment before dawn.

TABLE OF CARBOHYDRATE AND CALORIE VALUES FOR 100 GRAM (3½ OZ.) * PORTIONS OF COMMONLY USED FOODS

ABBREVIATIONS AND SYMBOLS

ANP ....As normally purchased
PNE ....Portion normally edible
CKD ....Cooked
Rw ....Raw
Cb ....Carbohydrates
Ca ....Calories
C ....Cup
CG ....Cocktail glass
BG ....Brandy glass
WG ....Wine glass

Foods are listed in order of carbohydrate value. Where value is equal, the lowest calorie count predominates.

---

* These tables are listed for comparative carbohydrate and calorie values of portions each weighing 100 gr. (3½ oz.). Special care should be taken to evaluate this in terms of portions normally eaten. For example, cola is valued in the list as having 10.3 Cb, and 41 cal. This is for 100 grams. The normal portion of cola is served in 8 oz. glasses which is, of course, more than twice the amount shown in the tables.

BEVERAGES, ALCOHOLIC

ALES, BEERS, LIQUORS, LIQUEURS, AND CORDIALS
(These amounts are not all measured in
100 gr. amounts, but in amounts stated.)

		Cb	Ca
Grenadine	CG	—	18
Absinthe (Swiss)	CG	—	49
Gin	BG	—	69
Bitters, angostura	3½ oz.	—	245
Rum, Bacardi	3½ oz.	—	245
Brandy, apple or cognac	3½ oz.	—	288
Brandy, cherry	3½ oz.	—	308
Rum, Jamaica	3½ oz.	—	490
Beer, imported	1 C	9.6	127
Beer, American	1 C	10.1	115
Ale, domestic or imported	1 C	12.0	144
Curaçao	3½ oz.	24.0	348
Creme de Cacao	3½ oz.	30.0	295
Chartreuse	3½ oz.	33.0	371
Benedictine	3½ oz.	33.0	398
Creme de Menthe	3½ oz.	35.0	375
Anisette	3½ oz.	35.0	385

WHISKEY

Scotch	3½ oz.	—	245
Bourbon, Irish or rye	3½ oz.	—	280

COCKTAILS

Martini	½ C	—	102
Manhattan	½ C	4.0	236
Bacardi	½ C	4.0	244
Camille	½ C	4.7	239
Martini, sweet	½ C	8.6	112
Old Fashioned	⅓ C	9.4	177

		Cb	Ca
Virgin	½ C	11.7	167
Daiquiri	½ C	11.2	199
Sazerac	½ C	18.6	321

MIXED DRINKS

Gin Highball	⅓ C	1.5	80
Gin Rickey	½ C	2.4	83
Gin Fizz	½ C	2.4	83
Brandy and Soda	⅓ C	3.3	87
Brandy Highball	⅓ C	3.3	87
Brandy Sour	⅓ C	6.2	98
Whiskey Sour	⅓ C	6.2	98
Brandy Fizz	⅓ C	6.7	137
Mint Julep	½ C	7.0	140
Sherry Flip	⅓ C	8.0	193
Tom Collins	½ C	11.0	118
Brandy Punch	½ C	11.2	118

WINES

California, red	3½ oz.	—	71
Vermouth, French dry	3½ oz.	1.0	109
Dry sour—Burgundy, Chablis Claret, Sauterne, Rhine	3½ oz.	2.1	71-80
Champagne, dry	3½ oz.	2.2	85
Dry sour—imported Claret and Moselle	3½ oz.	2.3	67
Sherry, dry, imported	3½ oz.	3.4	128
California, white	3½ oz.	4.0	90
Madeira	3½ oz.	6.0	130
Sherry, California	3½ oz.	6.7	144
Catawba	3½ oz.	9.0	121
Port, imported	3½ oz.	9.0	155
Champagne, sweet	3½ oz.	11.4	117
Tokay, sweet	3½ oz.	12.0	123
Vermouth, Italian, sweet	3½ oz.	12.0	174
Port, domestic	3½ oz.	14.0	173
Malaga	3½ oz.	22.0	174

BEVERAGES

	Cb	Ca
Coffee	—	—
Tea	—	—
Sauerkraut juice	0.7	3
Postum	2.0	8
Tomato juice	4.3	23
Buttermilk	4.6	37
Strawberry juice	5.1	21
Whey	5.1	27
Kumiss	5.4	52
Fruit punch	5.9	27
Ovaltine	7.0	73
Blackberry juice	7.9	33
Root beer	8.0	32
Raspberry juice, red	8.3	35
Eggnog	8.7	105
Ginger ale, dry	9.0	36
Grapefruit juice, fresh	9.8	42
Currant juice, red	10.1	42
Loganberry juice	10.1	43
Orange juice	10.1	40
Cola	10.3	41
Limeade	10.5	42
Lemonade	10.5	42
Raspberry juice, black	10.7	44
Grapefruit juice, unsweetened	11.1	47
Malted milk, plain	11.9	112
Cocoa	11.9	117
Apple juice	12.5	50
Cider	12.5	50
Peach juice	12.8	52
Pineapple juice	13.0	54
Blueberry juice	13.8	56
Currant juice	13.8	57
Chocolate	15.5	154

	Cb	Ca
Ginger ale	16.0	64
Grapefruit juice, sweet	16.1	67
Malted milk, chocolate	16.7	135
Grape juice	17.3	70
Prune juice	19.3	79

BREADS

HOT BREADS

	Cb	Ca
Popovers	27.0	194
Griddlecakes	31.6	200
Coffee cake	38.4	266
Boston brown	40.0	200
Muffins, bran	42.5	300
Corn bread	43.6	266
Muffins, cornmeal	44.0	273
Baking powder biscuit, cheese	44.0	510
Muffins, English	46.0	280
Baking powder biscuit	46.2	331
Waffles, plain	48.0	384

YEAST BREADS

	Cb	Ca
Gluten	38.8	254
Croutons, fried	44.0	457
Graham	48.0	262
Rolls, parkerhouse	48.3	240
Pumpernickel, all rye	49.7	236
Wheat, whole	49.7	246
Wheat, cracked	50.0	250
Rye and wheat	50.0	259
Rye	50.0	260
Wheat, fortified, milk	51.1	256
Raisin	53.0	275
Nut	53.0	292
Vienna or French	55.2	263
Rolls, French	55.7	279
Bun, cinnamon	56.0	304

	Cb	Ca
Rolls, average	56.7	299
Buns, currant	57.6	326
Zweiback	74.3	418

TOAST

French	42.5	340
Cinnamon	55.0	373
Plain	62.0	310
Melba	77.5	387

CEREALS

Cream of wheat, CKD	10.4	54
Oats, rolled, CKD	11.0	64
Farina, light, CKD	11.4	54
Wheat, flaked, CKD	12.4	60
Barley, pearl, CKD	12.9	59
Cornmeal, bolted, yellow, CKD	13.0	59
Tapioca, CKD	13.7	56
Hominy, CKD	14.9	69
Macaroni, CKD	19.4	96
Spaghetti, plain, CKD	19.4	96
Roman meal, CKD	19.6	104
Rice, white, CKD	23.2	103
Rice, wild, CKD	25.1	122
Rice, brown, CKD	32.3	149
Wheat germ	49.5	389
Bran, wheat, prepared	66.2	366
Wheat, puffed	75.6	371
Popcorn, popped	77.8	404
Wheat, shredded	78.7	369
Grapenuts	79.0	371
Malt	79.2	379
Cornflakes	80.3	359
Rice flakes	82.0	363
Wheat, toasted	82.0	376
Rice, puffed	83.3	363

CAKES

	Cb	Ca
Caraway cake	38.0	325
Devil's food	42.9	371
Nut loaf	43.5	360
Spice cake	45.8	312
Potato cake	50.0	358
Cream puffs	50.0	397
Doughnuts	52.7	426
Spongecake	54.0	293
Chocolate cake	54.0	438
Gingerbread	55.5	300
Poundcake	56.4	474
Cocoanut cake	58.0	329
Orange cupcake	58.0	362
Butter cake	58.5	388
White cake	58.5	388
Angel food	58.7	271
Fruit cake	60.0	385
Plain cake	62.1	325
Applesauce cake	63.0	300
Upsidedown	69.0	345
Jelly roll	70.0	357

CHEESE

Brie, American	—	285
American, processed	—	297
Camembert	—	306
Münster	—	318
Brie, French	—	321
Cociocavalla, Italian	—	346
Brick	—	360
Brick, processed	—	360
Pimento, processed	—	363

	Cb	Ca
New York	—	410
Cream	—	447
Limburger, processed	0.7	325
Limburger	0.7	388
Liederkranz	1.1	298
Swiss, American	1.2	430
Cream, full	1.3	530
Roquefort	1.4	391
Swiss, processed	1.6	336
Cream, English	1.7	367
Cheddar, processed	1.7	368
Cheddar, American	1.7	393
Cheddar, grated	1.7	393
Gruyere	1.9	404
Swiss, European	1.9	404
Gorgonzola	1.44	404
Parmesan	2.3	401
Pineapple	2.5	470
Stilton	2.21	459
Edam	4.0	305
Cottage, skim milk	4.3	101
Soufflé	6.0	297
Gouda	6.3	425
Fondue	10.7	210
Rice, macaroni, cheese, tomatoes (casserole)	20.9	200
Welsh Rarebit	22.0	200
Macaroni and cheese	22.0	232

COOKIES

Butter	43.0	462
Fudge wafers	45.0	420
Chocolate, drop	45.0	490
Walnut wafers	47.0	425
Oatmeal	48.0	337

	Cb	Ca
Lemon cocoanut	48.0	378
Date bars	50.0	305
Macaroons, cocoanut	53.3	492
Peanut	53.5	518
Macaroons, bran	54.0	294
Brownies	58.5	373
Molasses	60.0	400
Plain roll	60.0	400
Orange thins	60.5	351
Iced, thinly	63.4	500
Hermits	64.8	399
Sugar	66.0	492
Marshmallow	68.1	451
Ice Box	69.8	472
Lady Fingers	70.6	363
Oatmeal wafers	71.0	445
Vanilla wafers	72.0	436
Sandwich type	72.8	485
Sour cream	74.0	450
Iced, thickly	75.0	406
Chocolate wafers	75.1	443
Ginger snaps	76.0	407
Fig Newtons	76.8	343
Tea, Oriental	77.7	402

CRACKERS

	Cb	Ca
Soybean (cocktail)	1.3	303
Gluten	26.4	283
Cheese Ritz	56.7	491
Cheese Tidbits	58.5	421
Ritz	61.99	512
Peanut butter	62.2	480
Cheese sandwich	62.7	434
Egg	66.5	443
Cream	69.7	427

	Cb	Ca
Oyster	70.5	422
Butter	70.8	434
Boston	70.9	405
Saltines	71.1	427
Oatmeal	71.5	423
Soda	72.7	416
Whole wheat (toasted)	73.7	399
Rye Krisp	73.9	366
Pilot	74.2	385
Graham	74.3	419
Pretzels	74.5	362
Tea biscuit	75.5	432
Arrowroot	75.9	450
Animal or Alphabet	79.4	428
Triscuits	81.7	385
Water	82.1	374

FATS

	Cb	Ca
Mineral oil	—	—
Suet	—	852
Bacon fat	—	900
Beef drippings	—	900
Cod liver oil	—	900
Corn oil	—	900
Cottonseed oil	—	900
Crisco	—	900
Halibut liver oil	—	900
Lard	—	900
Olive oil	—	900
Peanut oil	—	900
Butter	0.4	733
Oleomargarine	0.4	733
Cream (whipping)	3.2	337
Cream (coffee)	4.0	208
Butter, peanut	21.0	619

EGGS

	Cb	Ca
Egg whites	—	43
Hen eggs	—	155
Scrambled	—	182
Egg yolks	—	352
Duck eggs	0.8	184
Omelet, plain	1.1	222
Goose eggs	1.4	180
Omelet, French	1.3	228
Turkey eggs	1.7	160
Timbale	3.1	117
Eggs á la Goldenrod	18.0	170

FISH

Codfish, fresh, CKD, ANP	—	87
Finnan Haddie, CKD, PNE	—	96
Haddock, smoked, PNE	—	96
Croaker, CKD, PNE	—	106
Codfish, roe	—	113
Roe, fresh, Cod, PNE	—	113
Alewife, CKD, PNE	—	114
Halibut, broiled, PNE	—	118
Shad, roe, fresh	—	118
Eels, smoked, PNE	—	119
Rock Cod, broiled	—	122
Roe (carp, salmon)	—	133
Sole, broiled, baked, PNE	—	133
Sturgeon, smoked, PNE	—	141
Herring, roe	—	143
Barracuda, baked, CKD	—	148
Mackerel, canned	—	162
Salmon, canned, PNE	—	169
Salmon, smoked	—	170

	Cb	Ca
Rock Cod, sautéed	—	173
Herring, salted	—	180
Swordfish, broiled	—	181
Red Snapper, baked, PNE	—	183
Herring, canned, plain	—	194
Tuna, canned, PNE	—	194
Trout, Steelhead, can	—	203
Herring, kippered, PNE	—	205
Bass, black, baked, PNE	—	208
Kingfish, baked	—	209
Perch, baked, broiled	—	209
Pickerel, baked, broiled	—	209
Whitefish, baked	—	209
Mackerel, smoked	—	212
Shad, broiled	—	216
Herring, pickled, Bismarck	—	218
Halibut, smoked, PNE	—	219
Bonito, sauteed, PNE	—	225
Caviar, Gran Sturgeon	—	243
Salmon, baked, ANP	—	270
Mackerel, fresh, sauteed, PNE	—	271
Caviar, pressed	—	288
Herring, smoked	—	290
Mackerel, salted, PNE	—	300
Anchovies, PNE	0.3	171
Lobster, canned	0.4	87
Lobster, broiled, PNE	0.5	84
Bass, black, fried, PNE	0.5	183
Crab, fresh, PNE	0.6	81
Shrimps, canned or CKD, PNE	0.8	82
Trout, steamed	1.2	111
Sardines, canned, oil, ANP	1.2	207
Crab, canned, PNE	1.3	99
Sardines, canned, tomato	1.4	167
Mussels, canned or CKD	1.5	108
Sole, sauteed, PNE	1.5	236
Clams, canned, meat, liquid, CKD	2.1	49

	Cb	Ca
Clams, canned, meat, CKD	2.1	94
Sardines, canned, mustard	2.2	195
Clams, meat, liquid, Rw	2.5	50
Scallops, CKD, PNE	2.5	102
Sand Dab, CKD, PNE	3.0	91
Mussels, solid, liquid	3.1	63
Abalone, CKD, PNE	3.2	236
Clams, average, Rw	3.4	77
Oysters, liquid and solids, PNE	3.7	50
Oysters, canned, PNE	3.7	50
Herring, canned, tomato	3.7	172
Anchovy Paste	4.3	202
Mussels, solid, PNE	4.5	96
Oysters, solid, fresh, PNE	5.9	81
Salmon loaf	6.0	194
Salmon, sauteed, ANP	6.0	236
Scallops, escalloped	6.4	137
Herring, fried	6.5	208
Pickerel, sauteed	6.5	208
Codfish, creamed	8.0	148
Oysters, fried, PNE	10.3	259
Codfish balls	10.5	202
Perch, yellow, sauteed	10.8	359
Crab cocktail	11.5	83

FLOUR

Soybean flour	12.0	292
Soybean meal	12.0	353
Gluten	47.2	373
Wheat germ	49.5	389
Lima bean	63.0	351
Bisquick	63.0	398
Bran, wheat, commercial	66.2	366
Wheat, prepared with fat	66.3	406
Oatmeal, Rw	68.2	396

	Cb	Ca
Buckwheat, pancake	70.0	345
Graham	71.4	360
Wheat, cracked	71.9	360
Pancake, prepared	72.3	344
Wheat, whole	72.4	360
Wheat, self-rising, all	72.9	340
Cornmeal, white	73.9	365
Cornmeal, yellow	73.9	365
Rye, medium	75.8	358
Wheat, patent, all purpose	75.9	355
Poyo meal	76.5	319
Barley	76.9	364
Corn, bolted, yellow	77.0	359
Wheat, pastry	78.5	354
Rice	79.5	352
Buckwheat	79.7	354
Potato	80.0	358
Sago meal	83.9	341
Cornstarch	87.0	352
Arrowroot	97.5	390

FRUITS

Rhubarb, water pack	3.0	17
Rhubarb, fresh, PNE	3.8	18
Cantaloupe, PNE	4.6	23
Muskmelon, cantaloupe, PNE	4.6	23
Strawberries, juice, fresh	5.1	21
Avocado, Fuerte, PNE	5.1	265
Strawberries, water pack	5.8	29
Muskmelon, all, PNE	5.9	28
Gooseberries, water pack	6.0	28
Avocado, Mexican Calavo, PNE	6.7	244
Peaches, water pack	6.8	30
Watermelon, PNE	6.9	31
Plums, water pack	7.0	30

	Cb	Ca
Avocado, West Indian, PNE	7.8	106
Blackberry, juice	7.9	33
Grapefruit, water pack, PNE	8.0	36
Muskmelon, Casaba, Spanish, PNE	8.0	36
Strawberries, juice pack	8.0	42
Apricots, water pack	8.1	35
Strawberries, fresh, PNE	8.1	41
Pears, water pack	8.2	35
Lemon, juice, fresh	8.3	33
Lime, juice	8.3	35
Raspberry, juice, fresh, red	8.3	35
Lemons, fresh, PNE	8.7	44
Limes, sweet, PNE	8.9	40
Grapefruit, canned in juice	9.0	40
Orange, mandarin, juice	9.2	43
Muskmelon, juice	9.3	37
Peaches, canned, juice	9.4	41
Blackberries, water pack	9.4	48
Grapefruit, juice, fresh (California)	9.8	42
Cherries, sour, water pack, PNE	9.8	43
Papaya, juice	10.0	40
Papaya, fresh, PNE	10.0	43
Orange, juice, all	10.1	40
Currant, juice, red	10.1	42
Loganberry, juice	10.1	43
Grapefruit, fresh, PNE	10.1	44
Gooseberries, fresh, PNE	10.1	47
Quince, juice, fresh	10.3	41
Raspberry, juice, fresh, black	10.7	44
Ginger, fresh root, PNE	10.8	64
Applesauce, unsweetened	10.9	46
Orange, mandarin, PNE	10.9	50
Tangerines, PNE	10.9	50
Blueberries, canned, in juice	11.0	49
Grapefruit, juice, canned, unsweetened	11.1	47
Oranges, fresh, PNE	11.2	50
Cranberries, Rw	11.3	53

	Cb	Ca
Oranges, Seville, sour, PNE	11.4	51
Apricots, canned, juice	11.8	51
Blackberries, fresh or frozen, PNE	11.9	62
Crabapples, juice	12.0	48
Peach, fresh, PNE	12.0	51
Pears, canned, juice	12.1	50
Limes, fresh, PNE	12.3	53
Apricots, sieve, unsweetened	12.4	55
Apple, juice	12.5	50
Cider, sweet	12.5	50
Loganberries, canned, juice	12.5	55
Cherries, sour, canned, juice, PNE	12.6	57
Currants, fresh, PNE	12.7	61
Pineapple, juice, fresh	12.8	51
Peach, juice	12.8	52
Pineapple, water pack	12.9	54
Orange, juice, canned	12.9	55
Apricots, PNE	12.9	56
Plums, fresh, PNE	12.9	56
Grape, juice, muscadine	13.0	52
Pineapple, juice, canned	13.0	54
Raspberries, canned, juice pack	13.0	61
Cherries, sour, fresh, PNE	13.3	63
Ground cherries, PNE	13.3	70
Figs, canned, water	13.5	57
Grapefruit, canned in syrup	13.5	58
Pineapple, fresh, PNE	13.7	58
Blueberries, juice	13.8	56
Quince, fresh, PNE	13.9	58
Raspberries, fresh, red, PNE	14.4	67
Youngberries	14.4	67
Pineapple, canned, juice	14.5	60
Apple, average, Rw, PNE	14.9	64
Grapes, American (Concord, Delaware), PNE	14.9	78
Loganberries, fresh, PNE	15.0	69
Blueberries, fresh, PNE	15.1	68
Huckleberries, fresh, PNE	15.1	68

	Cb	Ca
Avocado cocktail	15.5	135
Raspberries, black, fresh, PNE	15.6	83
Pear, fresh, PNE	15.8	70
Nectarines, fresh, PNE	16.0	67
Cherries, sweet, water pack	16.0	70
Grapefruit, juice, canned, sweet	16.1	67
Grapes, European (Malaga, Muscovy, Tokay Thompson), PNE	16.7	74
Kumquats, PNE	17.1	73
Guavas, pineapple, PNE	17.1	78
Grape juice, Concord	17.3	70
Pomegranate, PNE	17.7	75
Granadilla, fresh, juice, PNE	17.7	76
Passion fruit, PNE	17.7	76
Crabapples, fresh, PNE	17.8	76
Cherries, sweet, fresh, PNE	17.8	80
Plum, juice	18.0	72
Grape juice, commercial	18.2	74
Peaches, canned, syrup	18.2	75
Guavas, strawberry	18.2	83
Pears, canned, syrup	18.4	75
Grapes, juice, American, fresh	18.5	76
Gooseberries, can, syrup	18.5	78
Blackberries, canned in syrup	19.1	86
Prune juice, canned	19.3	79
Figs, fresh, PNE	19.6	88
Apple, canned, sweetened	19.7	80
Applesauce, sweetened	19.7	80
Grape juice, Catawba	20.2	82
Grape juice, European, all	20.4	83
Prunes, stewed	20.4	84
Cherries, sweet, syrup, PNE	20.8	86
Pineapple, canned, syrup	21.1	87
Apricots, canned, syrup	21.4	89
Grape juice, Delaware	22.1	90
Banana, PNE	23.0	99
Raspberries, canned in syrup	27.8	118

	Cb	Ca
Strawberries, canned in syrup	28.0	116
Cherries, sour, syrup, PNE	28.5	117
Cherimoya, PNE	28.7	124
Apple, baked	29.2	125
Figs, canned, syrup	30.0	126
Persimmon, native, PNE	33.5	141
Cranberry sauce	51.4	209
Cherries, maraschino, PNE	51.9	210
Prunes, dry, small	58.2	245
Prunes, dry, large	62.5	263
Apricots, dried, Rw	66.9	292
Figs, dried, PNE	68.4	300
Peaches, dried	69.0	295
Banana, dried	70.6	300
Prunes, dried, PNE	71.0	299
Raisins, dried, PNE	71.2	298
Pears, dried	71.6	299
Apple, dried	73.2	307
Figs, candied	73.7	311
Currants, dried	74.0	320
Dates, fresh, dried, PNE	75.4	316
Pears, candied	75.9	314
Pineapple, candied	80.0	327
Citron, candied	80.2	324
Grapefruit peel, candied	80.6	327
Lemon peel, candied	80.6	327
Orange peel, candied	80.6	327
Apricots, candied	86.5	350
Cherries, candied	86.7	351
Ginger, candied	87.1	351

ICES AND ICE CREAM

Custard	18.0	169
Plain ice cream	20.3	214
Chocolate ice cream	21.7	214

	Cb	Ca
Popsicle	24.5	202
Milk sherbet	25.0	135
Orange ices	27.0	108
Butterscotch sundae	28.4	213
Maple nut sundae	28.6	240
Lemon ices	29.0	116
Caramel nut sundae	31.0	219
Chocolate nut sundae	33.5	270
Fudge nut sundae	34.5	275
Pineapple nut sundae	37.5	235
Apricot ices	48.0	228

MEATS

BEEF

Steak, club, rare, CKD, PNE	—	189
Dried Beef	—	194
Round, pot roast, CKD, PNE	—	198
Round steak, CKD, PNE	—	198
Steak, club, well done, PNE	—	199
Corned beef, canned or cooked	—	209
Steak, sirloin, rare, PNE	—	215
Steak, sirloin, medium, PNE	—	235
Rib roast, well done, PNE	—	237
Rib roast, rare, PNE	—	245
Rib roast, medium, PNE	—	257
Chuck, CKD, PNE	—	260
Steak, porterhouse, rare, PNE	—	271
Steak, porterhouse, well done, PNE	—	275
Rib, medium fat, Rw, PNE	—	277
Hamburger, Rw	—	281
Neck, CKD, PNE	—	301
Rump, medium, CKD, PNE	—	316
Loin roast, rare, PNE	—	326
Loin roast, medium, CKD, PNE	—	347

	Cb	Ca
Flank, CKD, PNE	—	351
Sweetbread, medium fat, CKD	—	376
Plate or brisket, CKD, PNE	—	380
Hamburger, CKD	—	581
Heart, CKD	0.1	164
Tongue, canned or pickled	0.3	260
Kidney, CKD	1.9	240
Brains, CKD	1.9	391
Loaf, CKD	3.2	330
Liver, CKD	7.2	175
Corned beef hash	8.7	136
Dried beef, creamed	9.5	187
Round steak, swiss, CKD, PNE	17.0	299

LAMB OR MUTTON

	Cb	Ca
Sweetbread, CKD	—	100
Heart, CKD, PNE	—	166
Leg, CKD, PNE	—	265
Chop, rib, CKD, ANP	—	315
Chop, loin, CKD, ANP	—	321
Breast, CKD, PNE	—	545
Kidney, CKD, PNE	0.2	137
Loaf, CKD	3.2	330

LIVERS

	Cb	Ca
Liver, pork, CKD	2.0	153
Liver, calf, CKD	4.8	163
Liver, beef, CKD	7.2	175

MISCELLANEOUS

	Cb	Ca
Bouillon cubes	—	46
Bologna	—	218
Head cheese	—	243
Frankfurters	—	244
Sausage, polish, CKD	—	274
Luncheon meat	—	278
Sausage, CKD, country style	—	288

	Cb	Ca
Sausage, pork, CKD	—	320
Sausage, pork, link, CKD	—	350
Salami, PNE	—	427
Sausage, liver	1.5	258
Frankfurters, with cereal	3.3	201
Bologna, with cereal	3.6	217
Gravy, meat	4.6	100
Hash	8.7	136
Pasties	18.1	460
Poultry dressing, bread	22.2	167
Pie, meat	24.1	210
Poultry dressing, wild rice	43.0	295

PORK

	Cb	Ca
Feet, pickled, ANP	—	125
Feet, CKD, ANP	—	142
Spareribs, CKD, ANP	—	173
Chops, loin, CKD, PNE	—	179
Loin, roasted	—	209
Chops, rib, CKD, PNE	—	222
Side pork, fresh, medium fat, CKD	—	232
Ham, boiled, PNE	—	274
Ham, fresh, CKD, PNE	—	275
Ham, baked, smoked, PNE	—	279
Shoulder, CKD, PNE	—	366
Deviled	—	463
Salt pork, CKD	—	566
Bacon, Canadian, CKD, medium	0.6	491
Heart, CKD	0.7	190
Brains, CKD	1.0	269
Bacon, medium fat, CKD	1.0	599
Liver, CKD	2.0	153

POULTRY AND GAME

	Cb	Ca
Chicken, hens, CKD, ANP	—	110
Pheasant, dressed, ANP	—	125
Guinea hen, ANP	—	126

	Cb	Ca
Chicken, broiler, CKD, ANP	—	129
Duck, wild, dressed, ANP	—	131
Goose, CKD, PNE	—	153
Chicken, giblets, CKD, PNE	—	160
Chicken meat, light, CKD, PNE	—	166
Duck, fresh, CKD, PNE	—	169
Chicken meat, dark, CKD, PNE	—	170
Chicken, capons, CKD, ANP	—	174
Turkey, light meat, CKD	—	183
Chicken, roasters, CKD, ANP	—	186
Chicken, canned, PNE	—	191
Squab, CKD, ANP	—	199
Turkey, dark meat, CKD, PNE	—	205
Goose, CKD, ANP	—	216
Turkey, CKD, ANP	—	216
Chicken, potted	—	244
Rabbit, domestic, CKD, ANP	—	274
Chicken liver, CKD, PNE	2.4	152
Chicken, creamed	2.74	220
Pâté de foie gras, ANP	4.8	459

VEAL

Sweetbreads, CKD, PNE	—	118
Chuck, CKD, PNE	—	129
Shank, fore, ANP	—	142
Chop, rib, CKD, PNE	—	144
Chop, loin, CKD, PNE	—	149
Round, cutlet, medium, CKD, PNE	—	154
Shank, fore, PNE	—	184
Brains, CKD	—	393
Kidneys, CKD, PNE	0.2	137

MISCELLANEOUS MEAT EXTENDERS

Cheese, tomato, rarebit	2.5	222
Pepper, stuffed, salmon	2.7	155

	Cb	Ca
Chop Suey, American	3.6	270
Chow Mein	6.0	200
Tamale Pie	7.0	119
Enchilada, filling	7.0	205
Chop Suey, Oriental	7.1	94
Enchilada, sauce	12.0	113
Pepper, stuffed rice	12.9	123
Curry sauce, mixture	13.0	139
Macaroni and Bacon	14.7	197
Chili beans	15.0	97
Enchilada	15.4	157
Macaroni, tomato sauce	16.0	112
Coney Island	16.0	239
Spanish Rice, meat	17.0	205
Sandwich spread	17.0	362
Macaroni and Cheese	21.0	226
Pastries	21.0	279
Hamburger	22.0	203
Hot Dog	22.0	205
Meat Pie	24.0	214
Macaroni Croquettes	25.0	298
Chili Con Carne	32.0	203
Tortilla	61.0	292

MILK

	Cb	Ca
Cream, whipped	1.1	170
Cream, heavy	3.2	337
Cream, coffee	4.0	208
Buttermilk, plain	4.6	37
Goat's	4.8	70
Cow's, whole	4.9	69
Cow's, skimmed	5.0	36
Buttermilk, cultured	5.0	69
Kumiss	5.4	52
Evaporated	9.9	139

	Cb	Ca
Malted milk, plain	11.9	112
Milk shake	16.2	196
Malted milk, chocolate	16.7	135
Dried, whole	38.0	496
Dried, skimmed	52.0	359
Condensed	54.8	327

SAUCES

	Cb	Ca
English mushroom	0.9	35
Hollandaise	1.1	392
Mustard	3.3	123
Brown	3.5	137
Drawn butter	3.5	198
Tartar	4.0	514
Premontise	4.5	112
Hollandaise, mock	5.7	221
Béchamel	6.5	159
Cheese	6.8	265
Curry	7.0	110
Caper	7.1	151
Tomato	7.4	99
Egg	7.5	191
White, thin	7.7	189
Piquant	7.9	82
Cream	8.2	366
Soy	9.0	53
White, medium	9.4	201
Mint	9.5	38
Parsley	10.0	205
Olive	12.0	180
Bread	15.0	147
Orange	21.7	182
Vanilla	28.0	162
Lemon, regular	29.0	166
Brown sugar	30.0	120

	Cb	Ca
Cranberry	47.0	190
Butterscotch	49.0	245
Pineapple	50.0	203
Lemon, with egg	53.0	347
Maple nut	58.0	352
Raisin	58.5	261
Caramel nut	62.0	270
Chocolate	67.0	334
Hard	70.8	506
Fudge	72.0	362
Marshmallow	81.0	337

SANDWICHES

Club	10.6	236
Cheese, Swiss, rye	16.9	419
Sandwich spread	17.0	362
Carrot, grated, white bread	18.0	277
Lettuce and tomato	18.2	293
Cottage cheese, pickles, white bread	19.9	253
Cheese, American, wheat bread	20.8	405
Egg	21.5	299
Tuna	21.5	328
Cheese, American, white bread	22.2	406
Cheese, Swiss, white bread	22.2	410
Cheese, cream, olives	22.3	388
Cheese, cream, white bread	22.5	403
Cheese, cream, wheat bread	22.9	405
Cheese, American, toasted white bread	24.0	440
Avocado, white bread	24.5	289
Ham, minced, white bread	25.0	282
Ham, boiled, white bread	26.6	334
Peanut butter, wheat bread	30.3	500
Peanut butter, white bread	31.8	506
Date and Cream cheese	34.0	370

	Cb	Ca
Date and Nut	41.8	395
Raisin and Nut	46.0	433

SALAD DRESSINGS

	Cb	Ca
Roquefort	0.8	623
Chicken	2.9	215
Mayonnaise	3.0	720
Tartar	4.0	514
Cream	6.7	207
French	7.2	659
Boiled	8.7	133
Thousand Island	10.5	385
Mayonnaise, potato	12.0	663
Cream, commercial	13.9	391
Club	16.2	280
French, commercial	17.3	423
Fruit	18.0	149
German	30.0	354

SALADS

	Cb	Ca
Egg, mayonnaise	0.4	220
Tuna, mayonnaise	1.1	179
Chicken, mayonnaise	1.2	234
Lettuce, french dressing	1.7	83
Lobster, mayonnaise	2.5	162
Shrimp, peas, mayonnaise	2.7	165
Tomatoes, cucumber, french dressing	3.0	87
Asparagus, french dressing	3.2	97
Sardines, french dressing	5.0	284
Combination vegetable, french dressing	6.5	136
Perfection, mayonnaise	8.0	142
Pear, cheese, mayonnaise	9.0	225
Cole slaw (cream)	9.4	102

	Cb	Ca
Fruit, mayonnaise	10.5	146
Cheese, pineapple, mayonnaise	12.7	232
Pineapple, cabbage, french dressing	13.5	125
Carrot, Rw, mayonnaise	14.6	206
Potato, mayonnaise	16.0	167
Banana, mayonnaise	16.4	207
Waldorf, mayonnaise	17.4	241
Apricot, mayonnaise	17.6	225
Lima bean	19.2	158
Spaghetti, cheese, mayonnaise	39.0	312

PUDDINGS

	Cb	Ca
Custard	9.0	98
Gelatin, pineapple	19.0	87
Rice, creamy	19.0	111
Gelatin, lemon	20.0	85
Caramel	20.0	135
Spanish cream	20.0	148
Cornstarch, chocolate souffle	21.0	266
Tapioca cream	22.0	135
Cornstarch, plain	22.8	143
Rice, raisins	24.0	115
Grapenut	25.0	150
Jell-O	25.2	111
Bread pudding	25.8	170
Corn	27.0	136
Bavarian cream	30.4	296
Cornstarch, chocolate	31.0	215
Snow	33.0	145
Suet	33.0	198
Gelatin, plum	34.0	183
Strawberry cream roll	34.0	262
Tapioca cornmeal	35.0	200
Brown Betty	35.2	214
Prune souffle	36.0	164

	Cb	Ca
Strawberry short cake	39.1	234
Lemon chiffon	40.0	272
Chocolate, cold	40.0	355
Marshmallow	43.0	389
Apple Snow	44.0	180
Plum	44.0	238
Apple tapioca	46.0	186
Carrot, steamed	46.0	326
Fig, steamed	49.0	310
Strawberry souffle	53.0	313
Persimmon	55.0	272
Cottage	56.0	329
Date	64.0	399

PIES

Tamale	7.0	119
Custard	16.4	169
Chicken	22.0	304
Squash	24.0	160
Chocolate	30.0	220
Cream meringue	30.0	221
Coffee chiffon, without whipped cream	30.9	245
Lemon	31.0	223
Cocoanut cream	33.0	222
Apricot chiffon, without whipped cream	33.2	268
Pumpkin	34.0	200
Pineapple chiffon, without whipped cream	34.0	240
Lemon chiffon, without whipped cream	34.0	288
Butterscotch	35.0	275
Prune	38.0	240
Rhubarb	40.0	234
Boston cream	41.4	303
Apple	42.0	266
Black or blueberry	43.0	265

	Cb	Ca
Cranberry	44.0	267
Cherry	44.6	285
Chocolate chiffon	45.0	379
Mince	49.3	324
Pastry	52.0	576
Raisin	54.0	330

NUTS

	Cb	Ca
Butternuts, PNE	8.4	679
Brazil nuts, PNE	11.0	695
Pecans, PNE	13.0	747
Hickory nuts, PNE	13.2	715
Cocoanut, fresh, PNE	14.0	382
Macadamia, PNE	15.1	738
Walnuts, English, PNE	15.6	702
Nut and cheese roast	16.0	394
Peanuts, Spanish, PNE	16.5	613
Filberts, PNE	17.7	670
Hazelnuts, PNE	17.7	670
Almonds, salted	18.6	626
Pistachio, PNE	18.6	632
Walnuts, black, PNE	18.7	672
Almonds, PNE	19.6	640
Nut loaf, Walnut	20.0	274
Waternuts, PNE	20.2	88
Pine (Pinon), PNE	21.0	679
Peanuts, roasted, PNE	23.6	600
Peanuts, Virginia, PNE	24.3	587
Cashew nuts, PNE	26.4	609
Chestnuts, fresh, PNE	41.5	191
Almonds, chocolate	47.1	589
Cocoanut, prepared, shredded	49.6	471
Cocoanut, dried, shredded	53.2	579
Chestnuts, dried, PNE	78.6	378

SOUPS

	Cb	Ca
Bouillon	—	5
Consomme	—	23
Chicken	2.7	37
Julienne	3.8	47
Vegetable	4.6	36
Clam Bisque	5.7	64
Cream of Mushroom	6.5	102
Cream of Watercress	6.9	104
Clam Chowder	7.3	96
Cream of Clam	7.4	126
Cream of Asparagus	8.0	110
Cream of Celery	8.0	110
Cream of Spinach	8.0	110
Pea, split	8.3	66
Cream of Onion	8.8	112
Bean	9.0	69
Tomato, clear	9.3	43
Cream of Tomato	9.7	113
Oyster Stew	10.6	151
Oyster Bisque	11.5	108
Cream of Peas	12.4	134
Potato	12.5	81
Cream of Peanut Butter	13.5	248
Lentil and Tomato	14.8	99
Cream of Corn	17.4	155
Cream of Bean	20.4	169
Lentil	27.0	202

SWEETS

Chocolate bar	9.0	555
Chocolate bar, nut	38.5	533
Peanut nougat	50.0	493

	Cb	Ca
Chocolate, milk	51.1	551
Cocoanut creams	58.0	474
Parisian sweets	62.0	424
Nut bar	62.0	437
Frosting, chocolate	63.0	406
Peanut brittle	67.0	478
Caramels, chocolate, nut	68.0	516
Date, stuffed nuts	70.0	350
Chocolate creams	72.0	430
Figs, glacé	73.7	311
Molasses	74.3	339
Pears, glacé	75.9	314
Chocolate fudge	76.2	399
Gum drops	77.0	350
Praline, pecan	77.7	415
Popcorn, plain	77.8	404
Caramels	78.0	428
Popcorn, nuts	78.0	434
Pineapple, candied	80.0	327
Penuche	80.0	400
Citron, candied	80.2	324
Orange peel, candied	80.6	327
Lemon peel, candied	80.6	327
Marshmallows	81.0	336
Date creams	82.0	332
Chocolate nougat	82.7	422
Popcorn, sugared	83.0	423
Jelly beans	84.0	350
Divinity	85.0	407
Turkish Delight	85.0	407
Apricots, candied	86.5	350
Cherries, candied	86.7	351
Mints, chocolate	87.0	382
Ginger, crystallized	87.1	362
Mints, after dinner	87.5	350
Mints, cream	87.5	350
Stick candy	87.5	350

	Cb	Ca
Lollipops	87.5	350
Fondant	88.0	355
Butterscotch	90.0	405
Taffy	92.8	414
Hard Candy	99.0	396

SUGARS

Dextrose, crystallized	90.0	360
Maple	90.0	360
Brown	95.0	380
Corn	100.0	400
Granulated	100.0	400
Lactose	100.0	400
Loaf	100.0	400
Powdered	100.0	400

JAMS AND JELLIES

Apple butter	42.0	170
Jelly	64.0	256
Jelly, grape, plain	65.0	261
Jam, strawberry	80.0	320
Marmalade, orange	85.0	343

SYRUPS

Raspberry	40.0	162
Chocolate	48.0	252
Maple	64.0	256
Sorghum	67.0	268
Molasses	69.3	287
Cane or Corn	74.2	298
Honey	79.5	319

VEGETABLES

Mushrooms, PNE	—	3
Beans, soy, fresh, PNE	—	132

	Cb	Ca
Sauerkraut juice, fresh	0.7	3
Cabbage, Chinese, Rw	2.4	16
Cucumber, PNE	2.7	14
Taro, shoots	2.8	16
Chard, stalks, CKD	2.9	16
Lettuce	2.9	18
Chicory, PNE	2.9	21
Romaine	3.0	18
Asparagus, canned	3.0	20
Beans, soy, dried, CKD	3.0	88
Olives, ripe	3.0	189
Collards, CKD	3.1	22
Spinach, fresh, PNE	3.2	25
Beans, string, canned	3.3	18
Watercress, PNE	3.3	23
Dock or Sorrel, PNE	3.4	25
Spinach, canned	3.5	28
Fennel, PNE	3.6	24
Celery	3.7	22
Squash, summer, PNE	3.9	19
Tomatoes, canned	3.9	21
Asparagus, Rw, PNE	3.9	26
Tomatoes, fresh, PNE	4.0	23
Escarole, PNE	4.0	24
Endive, PNE	4.0	24
Mustard greens, CKD, PNE	4.0	28
Bean sprouts, Mung	4.0	30
Olives, green	4.0	144
Radishes, PNE	4.2	22
Tomatoes, juice	4.3	23
Turnips, CKD	4.4	22
Chard, whole, Rw	4.4	25
Chard, leaves, CKD	4.8	33
Sauerkraut	4.9	27
Cauliflower	4.9	31
Bamboo shoots	5.1	33

	Cb	Ca
Cabbage, PNE, Rw	5.3	29
Cabbage, PNE, CKD	5.3	29
Turnips, tops, CKD	5.4	37
Eggplant, CKD, PNE	5.5	28
Broccoli, PNE	5.5	37
Beet greens, fresh, CKD	5.6	33
Pepper, green, PNE	5.7	29
Kohlrabi, CKD	6.7	36
Bean sprouts, large	6.7	67
Chayote	6.8	32
Turnips, Rw, PNE	7.1	35
Tomato, canned, puree	7.2	40
Kale, CKD, PNE	7.2	50
Pumpkin, fresh, PNE	7.3	36
Okra	7.4	39
Carrots, canned	7.6	37
Beans, string, fresh	7.7	42
Chives	7.8	52
Pumpkin, canned	7.9	38
Leeks, PNE	7.9	45
Pepper, red, PNE	8.1	44
Squash, winter, PNE	8.8	44
Dandelion greens, PNE	8.8	52
Rutabagas, PNE	8.9	41
Brussels sprouts	8.9	58
Parsley, PNE	9.0	60
Nettles, CKD, PNE	9.1	65
Carrots, PNE, Rw	9.3	45
Carrots, CKD	9.3	45
Beets, fresh, PNE	9.6	46
Peas, canned	10.1	55
Onions, dry	10.3	49
Onions, green, PNE	10.6	48
Carrot, juice	10.7	45
Beets, canned	11.5	53
Artichokes, french, ANP	11.9	63

	Cb	Ca
Beans, soy, dried, Rw	12.0	350
Peas, green, young, PNE	12.1	73
Potato, mashed	12.9	115
Potato, creamed	14.7	134
Beans, chile	15.0	89
Potato, escalloped	15.2	100
Peas, creamed	16.0	133
Beans, kidney, CKD	16.4	92
Artichokes, jerusalem	17.0	78
Peas, green, average, PNE	17.7	101
Potato, fried	18.0	160
Parsnips, PNE	18.2	83
Tomato, canned, paste	18.7	106
Beans, navy, dried, CKD without pork	18.8	103
Beans, navy, dried, CKD with pork	19.0	117
Potato, Rw, PNE	19.1	85
Corn, canned	19.6	96
Garlic	20.0	99
Corn, sweet, green, PNE	20.5	108
Beans, pinto, dried, CKD	20.7	117
Potato, in skin, CKD	20.9	94
Horseradish, Rw, PNE	21.4	100
Taro, Chinese	21.5	96
Beans, lima, fresh, PNE	23.5	131
Yam, PNE	24.1	107
Tomato ketchup	24.5	110
Peas, green, old, PNE	25.4	138
Potato, sweet, PNE	27.9	125
Lentils, CKD	29.0	185
Potato, sweet, canned	30.7	131
Potato, french fried	40.0	274
Potato, chips	49.1	557
Lentils, dried	59.9	347
Peas, garbanzo, dry, Rw, PNE	60.9	369
Beans, lima, dried	61.6	341
Peas, cow, black-eyed, dry, PNE	61.6	351

	Cb	Ca
Peas, dry, split, Rw, PNE	61.7	354
Beans, kidney, dried, Rw	62.1	350
Beans, navy, dried, Rw	62.1	350
Beans, pinto, dried, Rw	62.1	350
Corn, dried	68.4	390